TOMB OF THE EAGLES

Death and Life in a Stone Age Tribe

John W. Hedges

WITH PHOTOGRAPHS BY MIKE BROOKS

D0048123

NEW AMSTERDAM
New York

To my parents

© John W. Hedges 1984
Foreword © Colin Renfrew 1984
All rights reserved.

First American edition published in 1987 by
NEW AMSTERDAM BOOKS/THE MEREDITH PRESS
171 Madison Avenue
New York, N.Y. 10016

First printing.

Published by arrangement with
John Murray (Publishers) Ltd., London.

Library of Congress Cataloging-in-Publication Data

Hedges, John W.
Tomb of the eagles.

Originally published: London: J. Murray, 1984.
Bibliography: p. 239
Includes index.
1. Isbister Site (Scotland) 2. Neolithic period –
Scotland – Orkney. 3. Orkney-Antiquities. 4. Scotland –
Antiquities. I. Title
GN776.22.G7H43 1987   936.1'132   87-20316
ISBN 0-941533-05-0 (pbk.)

TOMB OF THE EAGLES
Death and Life in a Stone Age Tribe

The Orkney Islands are justly famous for the exceptional preservation of stone-built tombs and villages, some of which are older than the pyramids of Egypt. And the remains of our neolithic ancestors found at Isbister breathe life into this great collection of ruins, and give us an amazing picture of the people who lived here 5,000 years ago.

In *Tomb of the Eagles* John Hedges describes vividly the tribe that had as its totem the magnificent white-tailed sea eagle. For these people the building and use of the tomb was symbol and expression of their identity. It was here that the dead joined their ancestors—but only after the flesh had been stripped from their bones. It was here, too, that offerings of food and goods were made according to the prescriptions and taboos of both group and society. Here broken pots were piled; fish, eagles and joints of meat mouldered; and the hands of the living sorted the bones of the dead.

But what of the people themselves? The 16,000 human bones recovered tell much about their stature, physique, illnesses, and life expectancy. Indeed, this unprecedented collection gives us a flash of insight into the structure of a *living* stone age society. That, perhaps, is the essence of *Tomb of the Eagles:* not dry bones, but a glimpse of prehistory.

JOHN W. HEDGES was born in 1948 in Kent, and studied Social Anthropology and then Archaeology at the Universities of Ulster, Sheffield and Southampton. He has spent more than a decade in archaeological work in the Orkneys, and is the founder-Director of the North of Scotland Archaeological Services. A contributor to BBC radio programs, John Hedges is the author of many academic publications, and a Fellow of the Royal Anthropological Institute. He lives and works in Oxford, taking frequent trips to his cottage in Orkney.

MIKE BROOKS is a recipient of the Archaeology Award of the Royal Photographic Society, and has been given the Aerial Archaeology Award three times.

Contents

ACKNOWLEDGEMENTS

The Isbister project as a whole has involved many and the contributions of all, I hope, are acknowledged fully in the text. In compiling this particular book fresh indebtedness has been incurred. Colin Renfrew, appropriately, has written a Foreword; David Clarke, David Fraser, Elizabeth Glenn, Anna Ritchie and Niall Sharples have all kindly permitted access to information prior to its formal publication; and Donald Davidson, Andrew Foxon, Raymond Lamb, John Love, Gunnie Moberg, Andrew Sanders, Violet Scott, Caroline Wickham-Jones, Bryce Wilson and Kevin Woodbridge have given valued assistance. The 'Tomb of the Eagles', as a phenomenon, is inseparable from the names of Ronald and Morgan Simison. Their ready collaboration over this volume is much appreciated and I particularly should point out that in writing the Epilogue and the account of the original discovery of Isbister free use was made of a tape and notes which the Simisons supplied for the purpose. The final line drawings for Isbister are by Frank Moran and those relating to the Links of Noltland and Skara Brae were drawn and processed by Helen Jackson, Mary Kemp, Ian Larner, Marion O'Neil and Alexandra Tuckwell. Figure 12 is by Alex Rigg. The other illustrations, where redrawn, are by a talented young lady who wishes to remain anonymous. The bulk of the photographs used for this volume were specially taken by Mike Brooks. The text as published has benefited greatly from the scrutiny and comments of Duncan McAra at John Murray; Ray Fereday; and Teresa Hedges. Teresa, my wife, also prepared the index and dealt with proofs but, over and above this, she gave me encouragement without which the book would never have been written.

J. W. H.

Illustrations

Plates

SOURCES OF ILLUSTRATIONS

1, 2, 3, 4, 6, 7, 8, 12, 17, 19, 22, 24: Mike Brooks; 9: courtesy of
Violet Scott; 10: courtesy of Ronald Simison; 11, 13, 14, 15, 16,
18: John W. Hedges; 23: Gunnie Moberg; 25: John Love.

Figures

Tables

Foreword

by Colin Renfrew MA PhD ScD FBA FSA

There are a few places upon this earth where the early human past, the long experience of successive inhabitants, seems only a few short steps away. Sometimes the landscape of low hills, silver sea and open sky can have a timeless quality, and the relics of that early past (the ancient churches, the burial mounds) harmonise with more recent testimonials (abandoned farmhouses and the concrete constructions of recent wars) to form a seemingly unbroken record.

Orkney is one of these special places. There, among the 'low green isles', stand the ruins of houses of less than a century ago where the way of life can have differed very little from that of the prehistoric occupants of the area, some 5,000 years earlier. Indeed at Skara Brae one can visit the remains of the finest village surviving from that early time of the first farmers. In Orkney, too, one may enter handsome stone-built tombs – the most famous of them is the beautifully constructed Maes Howe – which are among the earliest standing monuments in the world.

The finest public monuments of this early time are the great stone circles – the Ring of Brodgar and the Stones of Stenness. Today, more than 4,000 years after their construction, these gaunt upright stones are eloquent witnesses to a faith, or at least to ritual practices, which we are now beginning to understand a little more clearly.

These distinctive sites do not belong to the past of Orkney alone. They reflect, perhaps more clearly than anywhere else in Europe, the realities of a 'neolithic way of life', when food production – cereal agriculture and the herding of domestic animals – had replaced the economy of the hunter-gatherer, but before the rise of metallurgy or the emergence of urban life had come˙to transform prehistory into literate history. The inhabitants of Orkney must then have been largely ignorant of other lands, conscious only of the people of neighbouring areas, who led a life much like their own. Most of the population, we may be sure, had never ventured beyond the Orkney Islands themselves. The northern coastland of the mainland of Scotland – visible on clear days across the Pentland Firth – for most of them only hinted at another world. Their own was limited to their native islands. The most important places in this island existence were, no doubt, the monumental structures, mainly tombs such as Isbister, in which they invested so much effort, and which, in some cases, remain relatively well preserved to this day.

It is the great merit of John Hedges's book that it brings to life several aspects of the now vanished world of those early farmers. Starting always from a comprehensive understanding of the evidence, and with a keen eye for the lessons which the techniques of modern archaeology can teach us, he has been able to convey with great clarity what life then must have been like. The key to this fresh and persuasive picture has been the excavations at Isbister, conducted by the energetic local amateur archaeologist Ronald Simison. Their results have already been reported by John Hedges in a full and scholarly monograph, and now their broader implications for our picture of the society of that time are explored here.

The sea eagles themselves, which give the book its title, are an example of the way that modern archaeological methods can lead to fascinating new insights into the distant past. It is likely that the talons and other bird bones recovered at Isbister would have been completely overlooked in excavations at such a site only a few years ago: it was Ronnie Simison's careful exploration which brought them to light. And they were securely identified only because John Hedges had arranged for a team of specialists to work on the various finds from the tomb, including Don Bramwell who studied the bird bones. It was John Hedges himself who perceived their broader significance: these are no fortuitous inclusion within the tomb, but the result of deliberate acts, undoubtedly symbolic, by those using it to bury their dead. As he suggests, they raise the whole question of the use of a specific animal or bird species as a kind of totem, by the population of one particular territory, perhaps in order to emphasise their group identity. We begin to catch a glimmer of the beliefs and superstitions of four millenniums ago. When one looks for it, as John Hedges has done, there is other evidence for such behaviour in early Orkney. From such crucial insights as these the past is illuminated for us, a coherent picture built up.

Like any good work of archaeological reconstruction, this has had to combine the critical sobriety of the research scientist with the imagination and insight of the gifted writer. John Hedges is a scholar and an energetic field archaeologist. In this work he has given us a splendid evocation of that far-off world of the Stone Age farmers of Europe; a world which, in Orkney, sometimes feels not an entirely remote era, but one that is tantalisingly near, removed from us only by the passing of a few generations of fishermen and farmers.

Colin Renfrew
DISNEY PROFESSOR OF ARCHAEOLOGY
DEPARTMENT OF ARCHAEOLOGY
UNIVERSITY OF CAMBRIDGE
15 March 1984

1 · A Fertile Land

Those low green isles

Orkney is a place of unique fascination, inadequately described as a cluster of islands off the very north-eastern tip of Scotland. Few who visit escape its enchantment and indeed some stay – as they have done through the centuries. Succeeding generations have become the people of Orkney, the Orcadians, a friendly and distinctive island race with a rightful pride in their heritage and a sense of identity which survives exile from the islands of their birth. Whether one has the statutory three generations in the kirkyard or is just a visitor Orkney is a place one leaves with regret.

This book is about the first settlers Orkney ever had; in fact, the first Orcadians there were. There is no doubt that they will seem strange to present-day eyes. Perhaps they will be thought more suited to recent Africa, the American West, Australasia or Oceania. But if they appear rather too close to us for belief it is only because one archaeological site in particular has enabled us to penetrate the mists of time as never before. That site is Isbister – Tomb of the Eagles – and it has effectively given us a window on tribal Britain of the New Stone Age. Before investigating this further, however, let us examine the background in its broader context.

We must start not 5,000 years ago but several million. At that time fishes swam where Orkney is now and their bodies remain to be seen, as fossils, in the Old Red Sandstone which almost totally makes up the island group. Apart from some on the island of Hoy this stone has the property of breaking along its layers of sedimentation and of therefore being perfect for drystone building – a feature made the most of by our first settlers (and their successors). Other rocks are rare but brief mention might be made of occasional volcanic extrusions for, as we shall see, these were put to an ingenious use of their own.

The rock base once formed had, however, to rise up, be buckled and sculpted by nature, and then be partially submerged again before it even slightly resembled the Orkney of today. The islands we see now are really the tops of a drowned landscape. As little as 45,000 years ago the passage of a glacier smoothed the contours and resulted in the rounded hills and undulating plains so typical of the island group; equally important, the glacier produced and left a layer of boulder clay. This, with later wind-blown sand and, ultimately, peat was to form the basis for the soils which are, and always have been, Orkney's main asset. Finally, some 13,000 years ago the last links were severed with mainland Scotland and one of the most treacherous of channels, the Pentland Firth, came into being.

The advent of man, however, was still far off. The effects of the last Ice Age were slow to disappear at such a northerly latitude and the islands would have just been a permanent snowfield up to c. 10000 BC. Gradually, as the snow melted, a barren landscape gave way to one of open grassland and heath vegetation. With increased amelioration of the climate birch began to colonise, then hazel and willow until by 4000 to 3500 BC the islands were covered by scrub woodland with an understorey of ferns and tall herbs and with occasional areas of grass. Such vegetation still survives in one particular place – Berriedale on Hoy.

The date span 4000 to 3500 BC is mentioned so exactly because it is within that time bracket that man is thought to have first arrived in Orkney. And with him there came not only such things as cereals, cows and sheep – which didn't exist in Orkney before then – but also baggage of a more important, if less tangible, sort. In short, he brought ideas of culture and of society. He came equipped with the ability to do things from lighting fires to farming and with notions of the proper relationship between man and man and, dare one say it, between man and the gods. There was change over the one and a half to two thousand years we are concerned with here, just as there were over the preceding millenniums elsewhere, but the point is that man came to Orkney ready made. How he used his environment, and the effect he had on it, the form society took, and how it developed, are the subject of future sections. Here we use our licence, slipping forward to the present in order to complete our initial familiarisation with the islands.

How many of those islands there are is a matter of definition for although the figure of sixty or seventy is often given this includes those which are nothing more than tiny holms or skerries. The major one of the group, suitably known as Mainland, divides the others into the North and South Isles (Fig. 1). The south-facing port of Stromness in West Mainland is Orkney's principal connection with the outside world, the *St Ola* making one or more trips a day to Scrabster in Caithness and the *St Magnus* coming less frequently from Aberdeen via Shetland. Kirkwall, the main town and the location of the magnificent Romanesque red sandstone cathedral of St Magnus, is on the north coast of East Mainland; its harbour is used chiefly for local traffic but its airport provides a global link. The principal North Isles – Shapinsay, Rousay, Stronsay, Eday, Sanday, North Ronaldsay, Westray and Papa Westray – are all served from Kirkwall and may be reached either by boat or by light aircraft. The South Isles enclose Scapa Flow, the former naval anchorage; and since the Second World War the easternmost two, Burray and South Ronaldsay, have been connected by the defensive Churchill Barriers and may be reached by car from Mainland. Their western counterparts, Hoy and Flotta, must still be approached by boat or plane, traffic with the latter now being frequent in consequence of its connection with the handling of oil piped from the North Sea. None of the islands is enormous and even on Mainland it is possible to reach all destinations of interest by bicycle.

The general impression of Orkney is of low green isles (Pl. 1), most of the land being given over to pasture for cattle and, to a

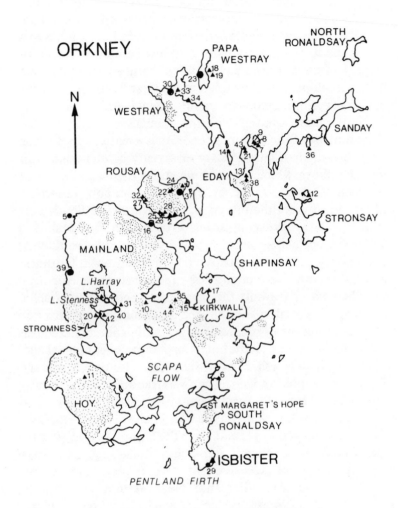

ORKNEY

N

neolithic habitation

henge

land over 60 m

chambered tomb

other sites

lesser extent, sheep. Some crops are grown but agriculture is directed primarily towards the production of winter feed. Trees are a rarity found only in sheltered positions and, wherever a person may be, horizons are wide with the sea never far out of sight. The best place to view the islands as a whole is to the west of Kirkwall where the Ward Hill rises to a height of over 250 m. There are comparable and lesser hills on the other islands but, generally speaking, change in contour is gradual and the landscape rounded. The one exception is Hoy, the red cliffs of which are among the highest in the British Isles. With a maximum height of almost 500 m the greater part of this island is bleak, barren and only scantily populated; for all that it is beautiful. There are other cliffs but for the most part the shoreline of Orkney is low and rocky with occasional sandy beaches.

The climate is very much part of Orkney's character and, indeed, the moods of the weather can transform the landscape not only from day to day but within hours or minutes. Perhaps most noticeable is the persistent wind. We can be forgiven for thinking this to be always present for meteorological records show that the air is only still less than 3 per cent of the time. The air movement can be as light as a summer breeze but for one day in twenty wind speeds average in excess of 30 mph and the equinoctial gales of March and September are in themselves a memorable experience. The Churchill Barriers are often

---

Fig. 1   Orkney: the location of places mentioned in the text:

1 Bigland Round	16 Gurness	31 Maes Howe
2 Blackhammer	17 Head of Work	32 Midhowe (tomb & broch)
3 Bookan	18 Holm of Papa Westray N	33 Pierowall Quarry
4 Brodgar	19 Holm of Papa Westray S	34 Point of Cott
5 Brough of Birsay	20 Howe	35 Quanterness
6 Burray	21 Huntersquoy	36 Quoyness
7 Calf of Eday SE	22 Kierfea hill	37 Rinyo
8 Calf of Eday NW	23 Knap of Howar	38 Sandyhill Smithy
9 Calf of Eday Long	24 Knowe of Craie	39 Skara Brae
10 Cuween Hill	25 Knowe of Lairo	40 Stones of Stenness
11 Dwarfie Stane	26 Knowe of Ramsay	41 Taversoe Tuick
12 Earl's Knoll	27 Knowe of Rowiegar	42 Unstan
13 Eday Church	28 Knowe of Yarso	43 Vinquoy Hill
14 Fara	29 Liddle	44 Wideford Hill
15 Grain	30 Links of Noltland	

impassable, the Northern Isles cut off, hen houses and their occupants have been blown out to sea, and it is occasionally difficult – and dangerous – to walk outside. Rain, too, plays its part for though the total annual fall is only moderate it does have a tendency to arrive horizontally. It is Orkney's maritime position at the junction of the North Sea and the Atlantic Ocean that brings about this inclemency but the sea also acts as a temperature buffer, snow rarely lying in winter and freezing point being reached only infrequently. The well-spaced rainfall, mild winters and reasonable summer temperatures are of great benefit agriculturally but so too is the long growing season that proceeds from the islands' northerly latitude. Being on a parallel with Bergen in Norway, the winters are dark – there are only five or six hours of dull daylight in December – but the summers are correspondingly light. On midsummer's day the sun rises shortly after three and does not set until just before ten and even the few hours of 'night' are so light that one is able to read outside without discomfort.

The population of Orkney today, as in the past, is essentially rural. Six thousand of the total of 18,000 live in Kirkwall or Stromness but the principal business of these towns is with the countryside surrounding them. Typical Orcadians live and work on their own small farms, chiefly producing beef and mutton for export. Whether in town or country they are warm people with an attractive and distinctive accent whose lives lack the hurry and pressures which are so much a part of modern-day life elsewhere. Orkney is certainly a very pleasurable and soothing place both to visit and to live in. It also, however, contains an asset of national and international importance.

Monumenta Orcadica

The ancient monuments of Orkney are legendary for their numbers, their good preservation, their antiquity and, above all, for their impressiveness. For many visitors they are

Orkney's main attraction and even the casual sightseer soon discovers a hitherto dormant interest in the past. If they are Orkney's ambassadors they are also prehistory's. Every year more than 35,000 people visit the neolithic village of Skara Brae alone; that is twice the present population of the islands as a whole. Skara Brae is just one of more than thirty sites of all periods which, having been excavated, have been restored and kept open to the public under the guardianship of the Scottish Development Department. These, however, represent only a minute percentage of the total number of known archaeological sites in Orkney – which is estimated at around 10,000. This is not the place to speculate on the reasons why some of the monuments were built and why they took the exact form they did but we might wonder why these vestiges of the past have survived in Orkney in such an extraordinary manner. There are three reasons.

The first is the result of a happy coincidence of nature. Such trees as ever grew on Orkney were never large enough to provide timber for building but this deficiency has been more than made up for by the flagstone of which all the islands except Hoy are made. This material can be quarried almost anywhere with the simplest of tools; it breaks into flat pieces ideal for building with; and it occurs in varieties suitable for objects as diverse as roofing slates and standing stones. There would have been driftwood and, doubtless, it would have been used for roofing, as in the recent past, but the flagstone is so useful that it may have been preferred for most purposes. Roofs were made sometimes by either stepping in walls until the gap between was small enough to be capped (corbelling) or by supporting a mosaic of large flagstones on long stones used as internal pillars. Stone was also used for internal partitions and for a whole range of furnishings such as beds and dressers. The popularity of this material has waned only quite recently since the introduction of cheap wooden furniture and, latterly, cement. There is much truth in the jest that the Stone Age in Orkney lasted until the first decades of the nineteenth century – as a look at a house of that date will show. What this means to us is that things built by man will survive, albeit in a derelict form, unless they have been interfered with. The latter is less likely in Orkney than elsewhere because of the ready availability of fresh building materials. But there have been other factors.

In more southern areas of Britain the rate of destruction of our archaeological heritage has become a recognised cause for concern. Roughly speaking, the rate is proportional to what we might like to think of as progress or modernisation and, of course, the impact of that on Orkney has been relatively slight. There have never been any canals, railways, motorways, large extractive industries, or sprawling conurbations and, as with other rural areas, the main threat has been agricultural. Even here Orkney has done well. Methods have been traditional – with the tractor coming only in numbers after the Second World War – and land is still worked in small units and with an increasing tendency for it to be left as pasture. The situation in rural Orkney is far removed from that in areas where there is relentless ploughing over large open acreages. Additionally, as will later be seen, the higher land in Orkney ceased to be of use to man at the end of the neolithic period and this therefore survived as a fossilised archaeological landscape, though much of it has been improved in the last fifty years. Once the point has been made that the ancient monuments of Orkney have survived better than those in less fortunate areas it must be stressed that there is no room for complacency. The sites of Orkney, because of their better preservation, are of international importance and the toll of agriculture is no less deadly for its slowness while the effect of winter gales on coastal sites can be catastrophic.

It is to be hoped that the value of the archaeological sites of Orkney will be generally appreciated now and that they will be left undamaged on that account. There was, however, another reason why they were not disturbed in the past and to understand this we must go back at least to the arrival of the Norse settlers of the ninth century AD. They brought with them from

Scandinavia their own ideas of the supernatural, of gods, giants, trolls, and other legendary beings, and it is perhaps not surprising that these became associated with the otherwise inexplicable ancient remains. Standing stones were giants who had been caught by the morning sun and petrified – though there are two which are known to go to a neighbouring loch for a drink still in the early hours of New Year's morning. Similarly the Dwarfie Stane on Hoy (Pl. 2) – a great isolated block with a carved-out chamber – was recorded in the sixteenth century as having been the abode of giants, though its name might imply otherwise. Some monuments became the object of great reverence. If one eighteenth-century authority is to be believed the two stone circles of Orkney, Brodgar (Pl. 3) and Stenness (Pl. 4), were known respectively as the Temple of the Sun and the Temple of the Moon and it was there that young men and women made their vows and prayed to Woden. Certainly the holed Odin stone, once situated between the circles, was the scene of such vows and of hoped-for miracle cures up until 1814, when it was pulled down by an unusually vandalistic farmer.

But these monuments are out of the ordinary, set apart from the more mundane mounds with which Orkney is littered. According to the folklorist, the late Ernest Marwick, a reverence for these can be traced back to the homeland of the Norse immigrants. There mounds were raised over the dead founders of farms and the ghosts of these somewhat capricious benefactors were appeased at intervals with offerings of produce. The mounds of Orkney were obviously viewed in the same light by the incomers for almost all had their mound dweller, or hogboon (Old Norse *haug-búinn*), and offerings of milk, wine, etc. were made up to the mid nineteenth century in order either to avoid misfortunes of various sorts or to bring luck, as on the occasion of weddings. The inhabitants of mounds were sometimes alternatively thought of as trolls, a mischievous race best avoided by man. If they weren't stealing human brides or babies they were causing illnesses and if they tired of that they passed the time with the music of fiddlers they had lured into their homes. Mounds and ancient sites in general are still loosely thought of as having been the habitations of the 'peedie [small] folk' and it is very interesting that they are spoken of as 'Picts' (e.g. Picts' hooses), these being the precursors of the Vikings.

One way or another it can be seen that any interference with a mound was a foolish undertaking. How foolish is shown by the following example, which was written down as recently as 1911 by the son-in-law of the man concerned. The opening of a big knoll was swiftly followed by the appearance of the mound's guardian 'an old, grey-whiskered man dressed in an old, grey, tattered suit of clothes . . .' His words to the farmer, quoted in *Old Lore Miscellany of Orkney, Shetland, Caithness and Sutherland*, send a chill down the spine yet, particularly as they appear to have come true:

> thou are working thy own ruin, believe me, fellow, for if thou does any more work, thou will regret it when it is too late. Take me word, fellow, drop working in my house, for if thou doesn't, mark my word, fellow, if thou takes another shuleful [shovelful], mark me word, thou will have six of the cattle deean in thy corn-yard at one time. And if thou goes on doing any more work, fellow – mark me word, fellow, thou will have then six funerals from the house, fellow; does thou mark me words; good-day, fellow.

In spite of these perils, some sites have been wantonly destroyed, but more happily, others have been excavated. The search for knowledge about the distant past is the subject of the next two sections; it will be sufficient here to review the sort of early monuments that occur in Orkney though with a certain emphasis on those of the neolithic period. This spanned the time – 1,500–2,000 years – from the first settlement up to around 2000 BC.

It seems most appropriate to start with the chambered tombs. According to a recent listing by David Fraser there are probably seventy-six of these known. With one or two notable exceptions they all seem to have been made of stone throughout and, as we see them today, they exist as mounds which contain a chamber approached by a low, narrow passage. They are particularly well represented among the monuments open to the public and, in addition to Isbister, there are eleven which are all well worth visiting. The most striking is without doubt Maes Howe (Pl. 5 & 6), first seen as a prominent green knoll on the left hand side of the Stromness to Kirkwall road, close to the two stone circles at the southern junction of the Lochs of Stenness and Harray. The visitor, having negotiated the long entrance passage, comes into a chamber which is breathtaking in its construction. The concept involved and the craftsmanship displayed are equally spectacular. The tomb as a whole has been described by Anna and Graham Ritchie in their guide, *The Ancient Monuments of Orkney*, as 'one of the greatest architectural achievements of the prehistoric peoples of Scotland'.

But even the more pedestrian of the tombs are extraordinary. They are some of the oldest standing buildings in the world and it is all the more amazing that where subsidiary chambers exist their roofs are often intact. In several places, as at Maes Howe, the main chambers have now been capped and this gives a very successful impression of what it was like to be inside one of these curious structures. My personal favourite is Cuween Hill, near Finstown, since I think this comes closest to replicating the original. The entrance passage is constricted and wet and the chamber can be examined only a bit at a time with the dim and faltering torch provided. It is cold, damp, black and very silent. There is no shortage of atmosphere. Other tombs that are open are Unstan and Wideford Hill on Mainland; Quoyness on Sanday; one on the Holm of Papa Westray; and Blackhammer, Yarso, Midhowe and Taversoe Tuick on Rousay. We must also include here the Dwarfie Stane on Hoy for it is commonly thought to have functioned as a tomb of the period.

In turning from the tombs to the settlements of the same age we must be careful not to let the riches of Orkney make us complacent. It is unusual for four settlements of neolithic date to be known in so small an area, and quite unprecedented for two to be in such good condition as to be open to the public. The most spectacular, and accessible, of these is Skara Brae, set against the beautiful Bay of Skaill on the west coast of Mainland. It is a site in a superior category, being one of the few in the British Isles to appear by name on even small scale maps. The visitor cannot fail to be impressed as he or she looks down from the height of the almost complete wall heads into the huddled rooms below. They are so much more than just buildings; they are the homes of families, each complete with hearths, beds and other furnishings. The huddle, too, is more than that; it is a village with a covered passage linking its component dwellings.

The second settlement that can be seen, Knap of Howar, is much less easily accessible, being situated on the small northern island of Papa Westray. There are only two conjoined buildings there but these, too, contain the remains of stone partitions and furnishings and, though the walls may not be quite as high, the lintels are still preserved above the doors. There is also the added satisfaction here of being able to wander around inside, a privilege it would be impossible to extend to the thousands of visitors to its sister site.

Orkney's two stone circles – the Ring of Brodgar and the Stones of Stenness – belong to the later part of the neolithic period. Lying north and south of the Bridge of Brodgar on the narrow strip of land between the Lochs of Stenness and Harray they are at the heart of a dense cluster of ancient monuments which include standing stones, burial mounds and Maes Howe (Fig. 2). The area, like its English counterparts at Stonehenge and Avebury, was obviously one of great importance in prehistory. The Ring of Brodgar is on a grand scale, with what survives of some sixty stones standing in a great circle on the heath. The diameter of the more verdantly set Stones of Stenness is small by comparison but that makes the height of the three stones that remain of the original twelve seem even more extraordinary. Whether viewed close to or as part of the land-

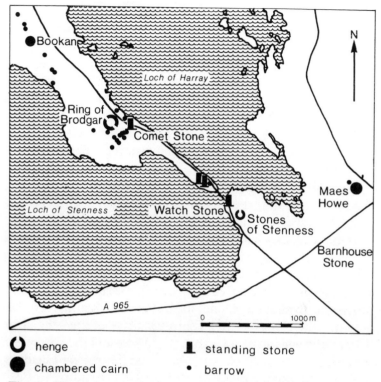

O henge   I standing stone

● chambered cairn   • barrow

Fig. 2 The dense concentration of impressive monuments of the Neolithic and Bronze Age in the Brodgar/Stenness area

scape, by day or by moonlight, these monuments are both impressive and thought-provoking.

The stone circles almost certainly continued in use beyond 2000 BC into the earlier part of the Bronze Age. The same is probably true for the less explicable solitary standing stones which occur throughout the islands. During this period there were very noticeable changes in burial customs and hence in the types of funerary monument that we find. The most obvious are the burial mounds, the barrows, of which the finest are in the Brodgar/Stenness area; others in Orkney may be comparable or so small as to be scarcely perceptible. But what is above ground

is only part of a story of evident complexity which involves a
wide range of flat grave types as well. Both occur singly and in
cemeteries, separately and in conjunction, and demonstrate a
somewhat varied approach to the disposal of the dead. The
habitations of the Bronze Age are also marked by mounds.
People in this period cooked in large water-filled troughs in
their houses using red-hot stones as a source of heat. The
shattered stones dumped outside grew into the tell-tale burnt
mounds, of which there are some 200 examples. The best one to
visit is that excavated at Liddle, close to Isbister itself.

We must now move quickly through the centuries for,
though interesting, the monuments have less bearing on our
present perspective. The seventh century BC probably saw the
introduction of both iron and a round house design. It was from
the latter that the brochs of the first centuries of our era
developed. Excavated examples of these high round towers
within fortified villages can be seen at Gurness in Evie and
across the Eynhallow Sound at Midhowe on Rousay. To this
period, too, belongs a rather contrasting type of site – the earth
house – and one can wonder about the purpose of these from the
subterranean confines of that at Grain, on the western outskirts
of Kirkwall. Very gradually we move out of prehistory. Little is
known about the early Picts, other than as a name first heard at
the end of the third century, but farmsteads of rickety, cellular,
half-buried buildings are coming to light. One was found
over the Broch of Gurness and has now been rebuilt nearby.
Similarly, the Norse immigration which started around AD 800
is at best described as a protohistoric event of which the most
definite sign is the characteristic long house. Such buildings can
be seen on the tidal islet of the Brough of Birsay, a site which
takes us through to history, the time of the first Earls of the
Norse Jarldom.

Even such a swift review makes clear the rich abundance of
ancient monuments that Orkney can boast. We now move to
how that source has been tapped, and to what effect. Again, the
emphasis is on the neolithic period.

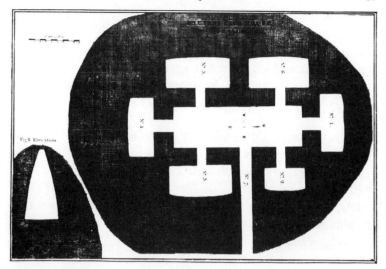

Fig. 3   Quanterness, as illustrated in Barry's *History of the Orkney Islands* (1805)

Past inquiries

Man is an inquisitive animal and forgotten buildings will always have been of interest. The entrance passage of the important chambered tomb of Quanterness (Fig. 3), for instance, was broached by builders in the earliest Iron Age and it is to be supposed that they satisfied their curiosity by crawling in and looking around. Such early investigators will have generally left little trace of their inquiries and the runes carved inside Maes Howe by intrepid 'howe-breakers' of the twelfth century are altogether exceptional. Among other things these relate the belief that the chamber had once housed great treasure and this and the famous dragon carved on the wall are reminiscent of *Beowulf* and reflect well the spirit of the age.

The first description we have of an ancient monument is that of the Dwarfie Stane which appears in Joannem Ben's six-teenth-century *Descriptio Insularum Orchadiarum*. Here the obviously local explanation is given that it was built and used by

giants whereas in writings of 1700 and 1792 it is seen, respectively, as the residence of a 'melancholy hermit' or of a monk
from the Western Isles. The influence of outside thought is
apparent here and we can see at a general level the introduction
of a rational approach and a historical perspective – though both
constricted by the horizons of the times:

> in many places of this Country are to be seen the ruins and
> vestiges of great big antique Buildings; most of them now
> covered over with Earth, and call'd in this Country *Pights*
> Houses, some of which its like have been Forts and Resi-
> dences of the *Pights* and *Danes*, when they possess'd this
> Country.
>
> (J. Wallace, *An Account of the Islands of Orkney*, 1700)

We hear nothing of excavation until 1795 when, in the *Statistical
Account of Scotland*, the minister of the parish of Stronsay and
Eday gave a brief and unclear account of the exploration some
three years previous of a place called the Earl's Knoll. This we
would now perceive as having been the remains of a collapsed
and filled-in chambered tomb; then it was a large grave, and
earlier inhabitants had to be of proportionate size. A much more
momentous discovery was a chambered tomb on the farm of
Quanterness, to the west of Kirkwall. Not only was this struc-
turally intact and relatively free of any infill but, more im-
portantly, there was a person to hand who appreciated what had
been found. To quote the Reverend George Barry from his
History of the Orkney Islands of 1805:

> As works of this nature have never been clearly understood,
> though they have excited much curiosity in men who take
> pleasure in studying the progress of the human mind by
> looking back to early ages, the utmost attention has been
> given to examine that Picts-house with care, to measure its
> dimensions accurately and to delineate the form of all its
> parts with precision.

It is also clear that excavation of some sort must have been involved at Quanterness: 'the earth at the bottom of the cells, as deep as it could be dug . . . being of . . . a dark colour, of a greasy feel, and of a fetid odour, plentifully intermingled with bones.' But Barry failed to ascertain either the purpose of the building or the age to which it belonged. Wallace, a hundred years earlier, had divided the monuments of Orkney into standing stones, burial mounds and 'Pights Houses' and Quanterness was just seen as one of the latter though Barry realised that it and others were scarcely likely to have been dwelling houses (he thought them defensive). While Barry tried to integrate the evidence of Quanterness into a view of Orkney's past he was fettered by his own times. The only reference he had was to Classical, Dark Age and early medieval authorities, though these were imaginatively and romantically supplemented. In leaving this period of thought and, to a lesser extent, investigation, we may quote Barry again:

Such are the monuments of that ancient people; who have been characterised as a tall, fair, comely, robust, generous race of men; with manners of such a nature and influence as to serve them instead of laws; discovering an ignorance of many of the useful arts, a love of some of them, and a contempt of others; subjected to a government, in which liberty and civil order were happily combined; and displaying a warlike spirit, that had seldom been equalled, and never surpassed; which was inflamed almost into madness by the peculiar genius of their religion.

Our story picks up again after a lull of half a century. By the 1850s, although the effects of colonialism elsewhere meant that the early occupants of Orkney were now pictured as 'naked savages', the age also brought with it its own characteristic obsession of exploring everything, of gathering information, and of publishing. It is an age of intended intelligent inquiry by men with antiquarian leanings and with sufficient leisure, money, and social contacts to enable them to pursue their interests. We must start with a Captain in the Royal Navy, one F.W.L. Thomas, whose ship, HM cutter *Woodlark*, was stationed in Orkney in 1848 and 1849 in connection with the drawing up of Admiralty Charts. In the latter year the officers and crew rowed ashore and, at the invitation of the proprietor, they emptied out a large and curious tomb on the tiny Holm of Papa Westray. Thomas incorporated the findings of this into a résumé, *The Celtic Antiquities of Orkney*, which must be accounted a milestone not because it introduced particularly new thoughts but because of its clarity and fullness. It should be noted that in this was the first survey of the circles, standing stones and tumuli of the Brodgar area.

Thomas had written his article partly 'in the hope of inducing some resident gentleman of more leisure and antiquarian lore to draw up a detailed description of these interesting Landmarks of Time'. His plea was certainly met with a great increase in excavation though the role of perpetrator became divided. The foremost gentleman involved, James Farrer, MP for Durham, was not indigenous but had a rapacious appetite for excavation matched only by his crude techniques, lack of inspiration, and general inability to publish. There was also R.J. Hebden, the proprietor of most of Eday, though he does not seem to have had quite the same flair. Last, and certainly not least, there was George Petrie, Sheriff-Substitute, Elder of the Free Presbyterian Church, and Factor of the Graemeshall Estate. It fell to his lot to make sense not only of his own work but also that of Farrer and Hebden.

Between them this trio was responsible for the excavation of around a dozen chambered tombs between 1849 and 1867 (including Maes Howe) – and it must be borne in mind that this formed only one part of their archaeological activities. Standard procedure was to have workmen break in through the tops of chambers and then empty out such fill as may have existed. Work was crude and speedy; bones were often merely of passing interest, small artefacts were simply not recovered, and what

Petrie jotted in his notebooks – still surviving – were largely memoranda about the shape and dimensions of the stone-built structures. But even with this level of information some progress was possible. The people we are dealing with here were not intellectually isolated but had a link with contemporary thought elsewhere through the medium of the Society of Antiquaries of Scotland in Edinburgh. Petrie was aware that a class of monuments which could be related to others in Ireland and Brittany had been brought to light in Orkney. Though careful to tighten up the definition of the term to suit, his pronouncement in a revolutionary article of 1863 was that 'the so-called Picts Houses are simply chambered tombs which have been despoiled of their original contents at an early date'.

Petrie and his immediate collaborators had taken us as far as they could but the Orkney tombs were thereafter seen as part of a general phenomenon. This is best illustrated by James Fergusson's *Rude Stone Monuments in All Countries: Their Age and Uses*, a book published by John Murray in 1872. Fergusson was an architectural historian and he brought together examples of such 'rude stone monuments' – which included chambered tombs, standing stones, and circles – from as far apart as Orkney and India in order to pursue his thesis that these represented an identifiable style of architecture, were connected, and belonged to the same epoch. As with all such broad advances there were blunders, which are obvious with hindsight – though some were to dog prehistory for a century. One of the first to be cleared up was the date. Fergusson, like others before him, thought of the monuments as being historic. But this whole way of thinking yielded to an increasing awareness that life existed before the Romans and that the vestiges of prehistory could be ordered according to whether stone, bronze or iron was in use for tools. 1886 saw the publication of *Scotland in Pagan Times*, a series of lectures given by Joseph Anderson, the gifted Director of the National Museum of Antiquities in Edinburgh, and here we read:

it is . . . with the sepulchral remains of the Age of Stone that we shall meet with a type of construction which is completely structural. We shall also find that the manner of burial, by the deposition of many successive interments (presumably of the same family) in one chamber, is quite unlike the system of single and separate interments in cairns or cemeteries which characterised the Age of Bronze. The types of urns associated with the burials in these Stone Age sepultures will be also found to differ widely from those with which we have now become familiar as the characteristic accompaniments of the interments of the Age of Bronze. The difference in the whole character of the grave goods is further intensified by the fact that among them we shall find no object of metal – but arms, implements, and ornaments formed simply of bone or stone.

The excavation that reflects best this state of knowledge took place in 1884 at Unstan, near Stromness, during what was otherwise a sixty-year period, from the 1870s, of comparative inactivity in archaeology in Orkney. The excavator, Clouston, was influenced by Anderson (who incorporated the work in his subsequent publication) and we see here a relatively ordered excavation, with a description of the contents as belonging to a tomb of the neolithic period and with the recovery of finds which included a collection of beautiful pottery vessels. The tombs of Cuween Hill, Firth, and Taversoe Tuick, Rousay, were also excavated in this period and though the crudeness of the approach was reminiscent of earlier decades the collaboration of Sir William Turner, Professor of Anatomy at the University of Edinburgh, is interesting.

With Anderson we see the tombs of Orkney as having been investigated, classified and duly slotted into their place in the order of things. A place shared in some respects by the standing stones and circles. For the moment there was little else that could be done. It is ironic, however, that Skara Brae had failed to be placed within this scheme of things. Known about since the 1850s, when it was revealed by a storm, it had been picked over for artefacts and then partially excavated by both Farrer and Petrie. Its date remained a mystery.

The next phase of activity in Orkney started in the late 1920s and continued through to the mid 1950s with a noticeable break during the Second World War. The influence of two government agencies was important here. The first, the Royal Commission on Ancient and Historical Monuments for Scotland, was charged to produce an inventory of the antiquities of the islands and its Investigators worked on this from 1928 to as late as 1937, though the findings were not published until 1946. Such a thing had never been done before and the result was an impressive catalogue of riches which is still of interest and use today. The second, HM Ministry of Works, had as part of its remit the opening and restoration of selected ancient monuments so that they might be visited by the public. This resulted, directly and indirectly, in the excavation and re-excavation of a number of sites and must be accounted a major stimulus – and one of lasting worth.

There were also the people involved and here, too, Orkney was particularly favoured. The most eminent was Vere Gordon Childe, Professor of Archaeology at Edinburgh University and, later, at London University. He was a man whose grasp of European prehistory has never been equalled, who was of international fame, and who brought Orkney to the position of pre-eminence it deserved. Then there was Walter G. Grant, a rich man through the whisky trade, who pursued an obviously deep interest, financing the excavation of a large number of sites on his home island of Rousay and then handing them over to the public. In his work he had the constant collaboration of J.G. Callander, the Director of the National Museum of Antiquities in Edinburgh and also a prehistorian of repute. Finally, there was C.S.T. Calder, an architect with the Royal Commission, who became one of the main investigators of the early prehistoric in the Northern Isles. There were others, but of less importance.

The greatest contribution of this period was to our

understanding of settlement during the Neolithic. Though enigmatic, Skara Brae was a spectacular site and was the first choice of the Ministry of Works for public display; clearance started in 1927 with Childe being present through the two seasons that followed. The wonders revealed merited three long reports and, in 1931, a book, but the period that it belonged to baffled even Childe – for the moment. The revelation came when he and Grant excavated an obviously similar, though very much destroyed, settlement at Rinyo on Rousay in 1938 and 1946. Here, sherds of a vessel belonging to the very earliest Bronze Age were found in a position which showed the buildings to be earlier. The conclusion had to be that these settlements belonged to the neolithic period, then put at 1800–1400 BC Meanwhile, on the island of Papa Westray, the landowner William Traill and his collaborator William Kirkness had explored two houses at a place called Howar. Thought to be Iron Age, the were to be the next surprise.

Childe's work at Skara Brae had been limited by the primary objective – which was to open the site to the public. Nevertheless, we can see several important advances, which set the tone for the other excavations of the period. The time spent indicates a great increase in care, as does the number of finds and the amount of faunal remains that were recovered. Photographs were taken, plans and sections made, and stratigraphy used to elucidate phases of occupation. Expert opinions were sought on different classes of objects and the reports incorporated in publications which were not only of a quality previously unknown but which also attempted to be farther-reaching.

Between the 1920s and the 1950s work was done on eighteen chambered tombs: ten on Rousay, by Grant and Callander; five on Eday, the Calf of Eday and Westray, by Calder; at Maes Howe and Quoyness by Childe; and at Wideford Hill, by Kilbride-Jones. In some cases the cairns themselves and even the area around was examined and it was found that, far from being a mound of rubble, these tombs were well-built structures with external walls that were meant to be visible. Further, some proved to have either hornworks attached or to have round them a platform or other delimited area. The position of objects within the chambers was noted, albeit only roughly, and careful work was rewarded by the recovery of impressive numbers of finds (mainly pots), and faunal and human remains – all of which were the object of subsequent study. Such care was taken in exposing human bones *in situ* that quite early on Callander and Grant were able to point out that 'some of the burials had been made after the tissues had wasted away' – a significant discovery.

The cumulated information on the tombs was to be incorporated in two major works of synthesis – Stuart Piggott's *Neolithic Cultures of the British Isles* (1954) and Audrey Henshall's *Chambered Tombs of Scotland:* Vol 1 (1963) and this and Skara Brae, Rinyo, Brodgar and Stenness have meant that the neolithic monuments of Orkney have become a key point of reference for the elucidation of this period elsewhere in Britain, and indeed further afield. One curious point is that, at this stage, the relationship between the settlements and the tombs was neither considered nor investigated. Grant's rather exhaustive work on the one island did, however, bring Childe to a perceptive conclusion:

> On Rousay there would seem to be almost as many family vaults of the Stone Age as there are farms today. Each vault might correspond to a social and economic unit of similar size. In that case the neolithic population would correspond to the present, less landlords, shopkeepers and artisans.

He had come a long way from hogboons, giants, and melancholy hermits.

The New Archaeology

In introducing 'the New Archaeology' we can do no better than to quote Professor Colin Renfrew, the major British exponent of the subject, from his revolutionary book *Before Civilization* (1973):

> The study of prehistory today is in a state of crisis. Archaeologists all over the world have realized that much of prehistory, as written in the existing text books, is inadequate; some of it quite simply wrong. A few errors, of course, were to be expected, since the discovery of new material through archaeological excavation leads to new conclusions. But what has come as a considerable shock, a development hardly foreseeable just a few years ago, is that prehistory as we have learnt it is based upon several assumptions which can no longer be accepted as valid. So fundamental are these to the conventional view of the past that prehistorians in the United States refer to the various attempts to question them, to attempt the reconstruction of the past without them, as 'the New Archaeology'. Several commentators have spoken recently of a 'revolution' in prehistory, of the same fundamental nature as a revolution in scientific thinking.

The catalyst for all this was radiocarbon dating – made possible by advances in atomic physics and pioneered in the United States by W.F. Libby. The effect of the dates, which have appeared in increasing numbers since 1949, has been such as to warrant a brief excursion here into the realms of science in order to explain the theory and method behind them. Unlikely though it may sound the story starts with the effect of cosmic rays entering the earth's outer atmosphere. These small, subatomic particles possess tremendous energy and one of their effects is to bring about the creation of an atomically unstable isotope of carbon with fourteen instead of twelve electrons. The two forms of carbon exist theoretically in a stable ratio and apart from the fact that it breaks down over time (to nitrogen) the radioactive type is in all other respects the same as the normal. It forms a bond with oxygen in an identical way to give carbon dioxide and is thus assimilated into the tissues of plants (through photosynthesis). Plants are eaten by animals, and animals by other animals, and carbon fourteen (C14) is therefore present in all living organisms. When an animal or plant dies its constituent elements and molecules usually go back into the cycle of nature but, sometimes, a part may be preserved for centuries or millenniums. Such parts – be they in the form of charcoal, wood, bone, or something else – when recovered from archaeological sites can be used to give an idea of the date of the context from which they came because the radiocarbon within them will have been breaking down at a known rate. The older any organic substance is the lower the proportion of C14 to C12. Dates obtained by this method have a statistical variability attached to them and are therefore quoted with what is known as a 'standard error'. Basically, the correct date has a 66 per cent likelihood of lying within one standard error each side of the central date; the use of a double standard error bracket increases the probability to 96 per cent.

This was all very startling, but there was a major hiccup. It was found that objects of known actual date – as, for example, from ancient Egypt – gave inconsistent radiocarbon dates. The root of the problem was that the proportion of radiocarbon to normal carbon in the atmosphere had *not* always been constant (as assumed) due to the effects of variable sunspot activity on cosmic radiation. Radiocarbon years were simply not the same as calendrical years and the dates obtained were therefore of less use than they might have been. The solution to the problem was thought out by another American scientist, Hans Suess. Tree rings are of annual growth and – a finding of vital importance – some of the bristlecone pines of the White Mountains of California were almost 5,000 years old. Some dead trunks were older still. By radiocarbon dating the rings of these trees – the earth's oldest living organisms – it was possible to chart out a relationship between radiocarbon and real (calendrical) dates. Since 1967 such charts, or calibration tables, have become increasingly sophisticated and archaeologists are now able to talk about things happening so many years BC or AD in a way that was not possible before. (By convention, uncalibrated dates are quoted as bp (before present), bc and ad. All dates given in this book have been calibrated and one standard error is usually indicated.)

Revolutionary though the ability to give such dates was, the effects of radiocarbon went deeper still; it undermined the very thinking behind what was then the accepted view of the prehistory of Western Europe. This is not the place to trace the development of the latter, but as the change has a vital bearing on the subject, it would be as well to outline some of the assumptions that had been involved. In contrast to our scanty knowledge of the pre-Roman era of Western Europe, the antiquity of the civilisations of the Orient was known about with a certain precision. The King Lists of Egypt, for example, went back to about 3100 BC and identifiable exports from that country could be used to date other civilisations around the Mediterranean, most notably the Minoan and Mycenaean. The known chronology of the East was used to date the emerging framework for the prehistory of the West. The fundamental thesis behind this was that developments in the one area had spread to the other by a process known as diffusion, such cultural transmission involving the passage of ideas with or without the actual migration of people. The theme of European prehistory was, in Childe's words, 'the irradiation of European barbarians by oriental civilization'. One had only to identify the effects of the ideas in Europe in order to get a date link with their source in the Mediterranean. There were, of course, refinements, one of which was the idea of typological development, or regression, as ideas moved further in time and space from their point of origin. Further, there was the concept of material cultures by which groups of people were identified by, or with, the objects they made and used – their artefactual assemblage –

and through which change and influences were observed. Prehistory was seen as a giant board game and the business of the prehistorian was to identify 'cultures', construct typologies, trace influences, and, ultimately, to obtain dates through links which spanned a continent.

Thus, the various types of chambered tombs of the British Neolithic, while elements of local cultures, were also part of a general phenomenon which originated in the east Mediterranean. Early Minoan examples on Crete could be dated to around 2700 BC and, allowing a certain time for diffusion and typological development via Iberia, it was thought that the idea came to the south of Britain around 2400 BC. Tombs as far north as Orkney would have been later and even more typologically removed. Similarly, the 'Wessex Culture' – the rich Early Bronze Age of the south of Britain – was thought to have been inspired by Mycenaean Greece and therefore to have begun around 1400 BC. The stone circles of Orkney and the large barrows around them would therefore have been put slightly later still.

The immediate effect of radiocarbon dating can be seen if we take just these two examples and look at them from our particular viewpoint. We now know the neolithic period in Orkney to have started by 3500 BC, with the Early Bronze Age having started around 2000 BC. The tombs there are older than the pyramids, let alone those on Crete, and our supposedly 'Mycenaean-inspired monuments' were erected half a millennium before that city started to rise. The links with the East were, quite simply, broken and suddenly the prehistory of Europe had to be seen in its own light rather than in reflected light. There was no longer any point looking to the Mediterranean for inspiration for that whole way of thinking had to be cast aside. European prehistorians had no choice but to start afresh and it was perhaps an opportune moment for thinking about the true meaning of the elucidation of prehistory. Diffusion, typological development, and material culture, if not entirely discredited, could be seen now to be insufficient explanation of the past. Besides, in one of their main uses, that of providing a dated framework, they had been usurped by the radiocarbon atom and the bristlecone pine. No, there was more to prehistory than these could offer and the better part of the New Archaeology is how that has been explored. Prehistory rose from the ashes renewed and revitalised.

Again, this is not the place for a major review but it is important that we look briefly at some of the means that have been used and more important that we understand the objectives that are now sought. It will be noticed that in their attempt to throw light on every facet of man's past existence modern prehistorians have searched other relevant disciplines for techniques and objectives. So diverse is the resulting subject that no one person can be master of all its intricacies and the trend has been for specialist authorities to come within the fold and to tailor their knowledge and research accordingly.

One direction of inquiry is the environment of man in the past and how he used and changed it. Plant pollen is virtually indestructible, being preserved even in coal seams, and analysis of samples from archaeological sites and from dated sequences in peat deposits or lake sediments will give information on surrounding vegetation at different times. This gives insight into the plant resources available, agriculture and husbandry, the impact of man over time, and even the climate. Then there is the study of the land itself, of available rock and mineral resources, of changing soil types, and of differences in sea-level and coastal outline. Recoveries from archaeological sites, of course, tell us most about actual exploitation. We find the skeletal remains of animals, birds, fishes and shellfish, the remnants of plants (usually carbonised), the tools which were manufactured and the objects which were made. These in turn tell us about hunting and gathering, husbandry and agriculture, technology and everyday life. The methods and results of such work are well illustrated in the following chapters.

Some of the skeletal remains recovered are those of man himself. We can look at his stature, physique, inherited characteristics and what he suffered from and died of. Given sufficient numbers of burials we can start to think about the structure of past populations, of such things as life expectancy, infant mortality, and of the proportion of the young to the old. The dwelling places and tombs that we excavate are few among many and the numbers known can be increased by intensive fieldwork and further projected by techniques borrowed from geography. We can examine the thinking behind their siting, consider them within their setting of a network of territories, sometimes hierarchically ordered, and, generally speaking, people a landscape rather than just focusing on individual monuments.

Prehistory now seeks to study man in the past on the same terms as man in the present. Like anthropologists and sociologists, the modern prehistorian wants to know how past societies existed and changed. He or she wants to look at their structure, or organisation, and to investigate their culture. Lest the latter be confused with the much more restricted concept of 'material culture' we must define it here and can do so by quoting the nineteenth-century anthropologist Edward Tylor. It is 'That complex whole which includes knowledge, belief, art, morals, law, custom and other capabilities acquired by man as a member of society.'

To acquire this knowledge may seem a near-impossible task, but in achieving this aim our chief asset must be the existence of a wealth of anthropological studies of recent and surviving primitive societies. In the same way that their geographical separation does not diminish their relevance one to the other, so their relevance to the study of past societies is not impaired by the distance in time which separates them, because they enable us to understand how social systems on such a level operate. Crude one-to-one comparisons of minutiae would be of little value, but broadly based parallels can be drawn giving us insight into aspects of the past unfamiliar and unexpected to the modern mind. In widening our horizons they aid our interpretation.

When work in the field resumed in Orkney, in the early 1970s, the New Archaeology was in its prime. Heightened awareness of what was now possible brought with it new directions of investigation and very much more advanced and painstaking techniques. 1972 saw David Clarke of the National Museum of Antiquities at Skara Brae; and Colin Renfrew, then Professor of Archaeology at Southampton University, at Quanterness, the tomb written about by Barry in 1805. The chief objectives of the first were to examine the midden left by Childe in order to recover environmental remains and artefacts and to relate these to an exact chronology for the phases of occupation. At Quanterness the aims were to elucidate the use of chambered tombs, to record with precision a very fine example of what was suspected to be one of the earliest stone-built structures in the world, and to prove the latter hypothesis by a programme of radiocarbon dating. This programme of dating was successfully extended by using samples from trenches cut through the ditch at the Ring of Brodgar and the supposed ditch and bank around Maes Howe and by searching out surviving material from tombs excavated previously. In this work the principal investigators had the assistance not of workmen, but of teams, most of whom had training, experience, and expertise in their own right. Work was slow and meticulous, three seasons being taken in each case. Archaeological layers were carefully removed, with trowels, in the reverse order in which they had been laid down and everything was recorded with precision in the form of plans, sections, photographs and detailed notes. The findspots of objects were plotted using three-dimensional coordinates and recovery was made absolute by first putting the dried soil removed into water (so that any carbonised remains floated) and then by sieving it. Work of such exactitude had never before been seen on an archaeological site in Orkney; this was, however, just the beginning, for the greater the pains taken in the field the longer the post-excavation work needed. It takes a long time to distil the essence from such voluminous notes and even longer for vast numbers of samples to be sorted, analysed, and reported on. Quanterness was in print in five years, in a far-reaching book entitled *Investigations in Orkney*; work on the material from Skara Brae is still continuing. This situation is in strong contrast to, for example, the opening of Maes Howe by Farrer; the digging must have been the work of a few days and the report was written, by Petrie, in the same month. This is reflected in the difference in the quality of the information recovered.

Such work requires substantial finance and in the 1970s this chiefly came through the Department of the Environment (a successor to the Ministry of Works, itself succeeded in Scotland by the Scottish Development Department) in the train of a national awakening to the importance of our fast-disappearing archaeological heritage. In 1973 the first of two seasons' work started at the Stones of Stenness and at the Knap of Howar on Papa Westray. At the former site Graham Ritchie, an Investigator with the Royal Commission, examined a large area of the interior of the circle, located the sockets of all but one of the missing stones, and explored the ditch and its terminals. The structures at the Knap of Howar, long thought to be Iron Age, proved on excavation by Anna Ritchie to be the earliest known stone-built dwellings. The first of the Ritchies' reports was published in 1976 and the second is in press. Yet another neolithic village, the Links of Noltland, was traced on Westray through drawings of sherds in one of George Petrie's notebooks and this has been the focus of major investigations, embarked on in 1978 by David Clarke. In a contemporary large-scale operation at the Howe near Stromness the North of Scotland Archaeological Services found a sequence of Iron Age and Pictish occupation to have been built over a neolithic tomb. The potential of Orkney for the elucidation of the neolithic period seemed inexhaustible but financial backing was to dwindle with the government cuts which came with the new decade. Both the Links of Noltland and the Howe suffered and the discovery of a magnificent carved stone in association with an unknown tomb at Pierowall Quarry on Westray could be met only with a holding operation under the direction of Niall Sharples, an archaeologist attached to the National Museum of. Antiquities of Scotland. The sole investigation currently in progress, that on a chambered tomb on the Holm of Papa Westray, is funded modestly through grants from the Society of Antiquaries of Scotland, the Society of Antiquaries of London, the Russell Trust, and the Orkney Islands Council. The tomb is very close to the Knap of Howar and it is the hope of the excavator of both sites, Anna Ritchie, that they will prove to be connected.

Isbister itself has not yet been mentioned but the principal excavations were undertaken in 1976 and therefore fit within the milieu of the New Archaeology. An extraordinary site in its own right, it helps to gel much of the information that has been gleaned from others. The extent of that information makes Orkney unique. More than three dozen sites of neolithic date have been investigated and, additionally, there are comprehensive records of all that are known to survive. In the latter respect we are fortunate to have not only Audrey Henshall's scholarly compilation of 1963 and the continuing work of Raymond Lamb, County Archaeologist since 1978, but also the recently published doctoral dissertation of David Fraser. Orkney is quite simply the best area that exists for reconstructing a comprehensive view of life in Britain in the neolithic period and, as we shall see, Isbister provides an ideal vantage from which to attempt this. First, however, we must look at how that site was investigated at the hands of its discoverer, Ronald Simison.

1 Typically flat Orcadian farmland with Hoy in the background

2 The enigmatic Dwarfie Stane on Hoy

3 An arc of the surviving stones of the great Ring of Brodgar

4 The tall, slant-topped Stones of Stenness

5 Interior of Maes Howe, from an old engraving in Farrer's publication
of 1862

6 Maes Howe, as seen by the approaching visitor

7 The cliffs at Isbister; site indicated by arrow

8 The cache of objects found at Isbister in 1958; the jet ring,
   discovered in 1976, is also shown

9 Visitors to the first opening of Isbister in 1958

10 Bones found in 1958 at Isbister and taken to St Margaret's Hope for
safe-keeping

11 Northern hornwork at Isbister with material dumped behind

12 Rude stone implements from the material behind the northern
   hornwork

13 The tomb of Isbister from the east

14 Post-cranial bones under the end shelf in the chamber at Isbister

15 Skulls in the side cell discovered at Isbister in 1976

16 Excarnated burials in the main chamber at Isbister; that on the left of the entrance to the side cell was lifted separately

17 Interior of the chamber at Isbister as it is now seen

18 Ronald Simison excavating among the human bones on the floor of the chamber at Isbister

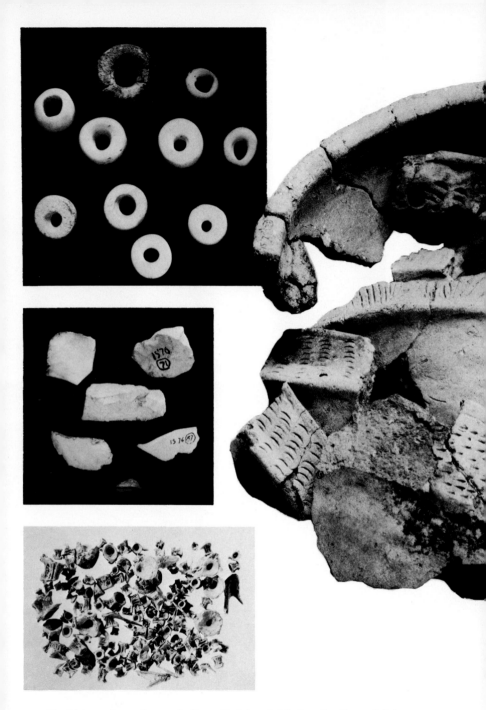

19 Objects from the tomb floor. *Left hand side:* beads; flints; fish bones.
Centre: Unstan Ware pottery

Right hand side: limpet shells with their apices removed; a fingernail-impressed sherd; carbonised grain

20 Nineteenth-century engraving of the interior of a Parsee tower of silence in India. The bones are put into the central 'well' after the flesh has been consumed by vultures

21 Nineteenth-century engraving of a scaffold burial of the Dakota American Indians

22 Hut 1, one of the cluster of dwellings which comprise the
miraculously preserved Stone Age village of Skara Brae

23 An aerial view of the Knap of Howar, the best example of domestic
architecture known in western Europe for the early Neolithic

24 Human bones from Isbister. *Top row:* osteoarthritic rib; lumbar
vertebra with marked osteophytosis; osteoarthritis of the upper
knee joint; Charlie – note depression across top of skull; *centre row:*
crush fracture of a lumbar vertebra; atlas vertebra with double

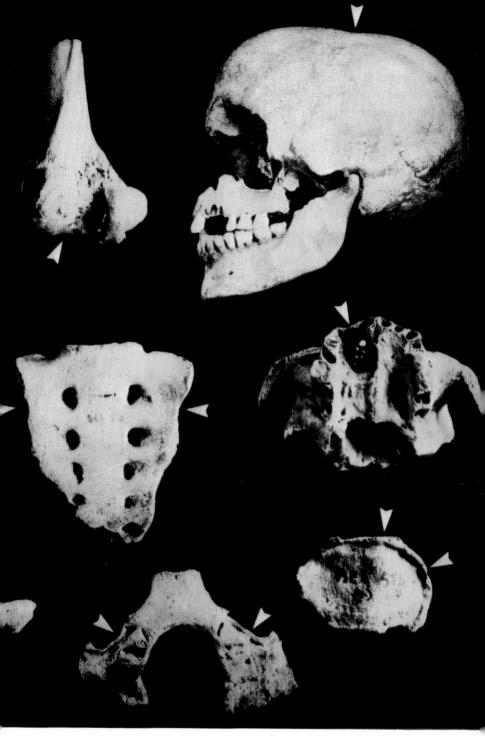

faceting; sacralisation of the last lumbar vertebra; oval depression
left in upper palate by a cyst; *bottom row:* typical skulls; localised
osteoarthritis in a neck vertebra; treble faceting of the occipital
condyles; osteoarthritic knee cap

25 A white-tailed sea eagle, Colla. Now reintroduced to Britain, such
birds may nest once more on the cliffs below the tomb of Isbister

2 · Excavations at Isbister

Discovery and first delvings

Ronald Simison was born just after the First World War, after
the Kaiser's fleet had scuttled itself in Scapa Flow and while it
was being salvaged and broken up with patriotic zeal. There
were no Churchill Barriers then and South Ronaldsay was very
much an island. His father's farm at Liddle was right at the
south end looking over the Pentland Firth to Scotland, and
some seven miles from the village of St Margaret's Hope, from
which boats went to Scapa near Kirkwall and to Scrabster in
Caithness. Life was certainly different then, though the school
for the South Parish was much in advance of its times, its three
tall rooms with enormous windows being provided by a former
islander who had risen to wealth in the Hudson's Bay Company
of Canada. Still, the scholars went there often unshod in
summer and carrying a peat in winter, having walked as many
as three or four miles over fields, heather and rough tracks.
Families tended to be large, houses relatively small and labour-
intensive; as in other parts of rural Britain at the time there
was no gas, electricity, running water or mains sewerage and
transport was, at best, horse drawn. His schooling completed
at the age of fourteen, Ronald Simison went to work on a
neighbouring farm. Thereafter he was to inherit his father's
land, to marry a girl from the parish, Morgan, and they were to
become the centre of a large family of their own.

Changes that had come in the wake of the Second World War
included not only the Barriers and tractors but a place in a
national market and the government-sponsored introduction of
improved agricultural methods. This ultimately resulted in
larger farms which were given over to cattle and sheep rather

than to the production of crops for local consumption. The Simisons were well ahead in this trend and by the mid 1950s the land of Liddle had been extended to include that of three other farms. One of these was Isbister.

Barbed wire fences needed to be erected on some of the new land and for this corner posts – or strainers – were necessary. Nowadays these are made from reinforced concrete but then, in the tradition of Orkney, it was common for flagstone to be used – though pieces of suitable thickness and length were not easily obtained. Ronald Simison had, however, noted a promising area of bare flagstone against the cliffs at Isbister (Pl. 7) and went one evening in the summer of 1958 to see if he could quarry what he wanted from the exposed rock there. In this he was frustrated but he had not taken many steps homeward before his thoughts were diverted. To someone as familiar with the land as he was it was evident that in going from the exposed flagstones to the agricultural land beyond he had to pass over a rise. This was most prominent directly opposite the cliffs and particularly here it seemed to make little sense as a natural feature since the tips of solidly set vertical stones projected here and there through the turf. Ronald Simison was pondering this when he saw what looked to be a piece of built wall going in a curve and, sitting down, he began to expose its outer face, pulling away the turf and rubble that lay against it. It was indeed a wall and, in a sense, the tomb of Isbister can be said to have been discovered at that moment. Old built walls are not uncommon in Orkney and I wonder myself whether matters might not have stopped there had it not been for a remarkable circumstance. The piece of the tomb's outer edge that he found was a fragment on the seaward side which had survived earlier quarrying; it was only a few stones high and, by sheer coincidence, it was also the spot where a cache of valued objects had been deposited in antiquity. Within the space of a quarter of an hour Ronald Simison had reached the bottom of the wall and had recovered a collection of objects such as any museum would be proud to display. There was a magnificent mace-head, ground and polished out of black and white stone; one black and two green-brown polished stone axe-heads; a flat sliver of smooth orange stone that looked like a knife; and a perfectly formed button of what proved to be highly polished jet (Pl. 8).

There was no doubt in Ronald Simison's mind that what he had come upon was Stone Age and the objects he had found were a natural source of pride and interest. He took them one night to St Margaret's Hope to show people in the bar there and another day they went down with him to the boatshed from which a crew supplied the lighthouse on the Pentland Skerries. The mail driver there took them to Stromness from where they were sent, on loan, to the National Museum of Antiquities in Edinburgh, being exhibited for some twenty years.

Things were happening fast. The initial discovery had taken place on a Thursday night and that Sunday, a day free from farm work, Ronald Simison and his neighbour and brother-in-law, Charlie Scott, took spades in order to investigate further. They were not alone, for news had travelled and quite a crowd had gathered to watch. The spot chosen for excavation was where the uprights poked through the turf and a little digging showed these to be connected by walling. Gradually it became clear to the excavators that they were going down within a narrow room – we now know this to be the north end of the tomb's chamber. We also know now that it had been excavated before – probably when the tomb as a whole was quarried – but this only added interest, for the material which had been used to fill in the hole was loose, and thick with teeth, jaws, and other recognisable human bones. These were duly put in a great pile at the side of the trench (Pl. 9) and the site having been discovered to be a 'burial place' the onlookers dispersed leaving Ronnie and Charlie still digging. By now the hole they were in was a metre or so deep and a lintel had been revealed in the northern wall. This was only appreciated for what it was when Charlie's spade went in under it and there then followed a short spate of feverish digging until the top of a small entrance had been cleared. The excavators looked in but could see nothing –

just blackness. Charlie, however, had a cigarette lighter which, thrust in the hole, illuminated a sight which was as strange as it was unexpected. The entrance led directly into a tiny roofed cell, the floor of which was covered with human skulls.

As may be imagined this caused considerable excitement and what was left of the fill of the chamber was rapidly taken out – the floor now being known to be less than half a metre below. Here, too, there were skulls, though damaged and dirty – seemingly in pairs against the walls and uprights – and there were plenty of other bones besides. Everything was left as it had been found pending examination at more expert hands. Ronnie phoned his brother in Kirkwall, a vet, who contacted Dr Hugh Marwick, a prominent local scholar, former Vice-President of the Orkney Antiquarian Society and a Fellow of the Society of Antiquaries of Scotland. He promised to come as soon as possible and meanwhile hordes of visitors had to be restrained from disturbing the bones – and even from taking them as souvenirs. On some days there were as many as fifty sightseers and these included a brother-in-law and a friend from the island of Flotta who came by dinghy and then bicycle.

In those days there was no metalled road to the farm of Liddle and Ronnie walked up over the fields to meet Hugh Marwick where he was picnicking next to a haystack with a visiting doctor from Edinburgh and his wife. Ronnie joined them, though he found the table wine offered little to his liking – he is prejudiced against the stuff to this day. The picnic completed, Ronnie guided the party to the cliff-edge only to find that they wouldn't descend into the hole but that he had to take skulls out to them. These were duly measured with calipers and pronounced to be 'long heads'. That was as far as Dr Marwick went, but he did inform the Ancient Monuments Branch of the Ministry of Works in Edinburgh of what had been discovered. In the meantime the site was still being inundated with visitors – including the police – and the possibility of the bones becoming damaged and disarranged was becoming critical. The Ancient Monuments Branch had, however, contacted the doctor of

South Ronaldsay, Dr Hooker, and he came out to Liddle with his wife and a student doctor with instructions to gather the bones for their safe keeping. Ronnie accordingly handed them out of the chamber, when they were packed in a tin bath, boxes and baskets, carried to the public road, and transported to storage in St Margaret's Hope (Pl. 10).

Next, Roy Ritchie, an Inspector of Ancient Monuments arrived from Edinburgh. He duly planned the revealed chamber and the mound immediately around it, took notes of what Ronald Simison said he had found, discovered four small fragments of pottery on the spoil tip, and made arrangements for the bones collected to be sent south. The floor deposits and smaller bones remaining in the chamber were left without further investigation and the excavations were filled in, an understanding being given that the site would be re-opened when other work then current in Orkney was at an end. The whole episode was then sewn up from the official point of view by a report in the *Proceedings of the Society of Antiquaries of Scotland* in which the structure and finds were described and discussed briefly. The bones recovered never were analysed, though a belated and unsuccessful attempt was made to discover which had come from the side cell. Not all the bones were there, however, for the Simisons had kept one skull, which went by the name of 'Charlie' and this was a symbol of their continued interest in the site – as well as being a rather unusual conversation piece (Pl. 24).

A profitable interlude

These first, relatively unskilled delvings sparked off a number of other excavations on unrecorded ancient monuments on Ronald Simison's land. Where Isbister differed from these was in the immediately obvious richness of what had been found and the fact that so much more was known to remain, yet to be uncovered. Let it be clear at this point that such activities would never be condoned in this decade. In the 1950s, however, we as a nation had yet to come to an awareness of the absolute breadth, fragility, and importance of our archaeological heritage and Ronald Simison's early work and the handling of it by professionals was a small part of this process of enlightenment. As it happens, the damage done at Isbister was comparatively slight for the descent to the chamber floor was within the workings of a previous excavation. Though we have no record of this it is certain that the floor deposits were disturbed and that the side cell was, at the least, looked into.

Isbister remained a tantalising site for two decades. It was certainly never very far from the thoughts of the Simisons. 'Charlie' was usually brought out when visitors came and as he sat on the sideboard and home-brew was consumed conversation often turned to the tomb at the cliff-edge. The most persistent element of such conversation was what a pity it was that work had not been taken any further. This was an obsession which nagged and as years passed it did not dim, but increased. The general feeling was that, the discovery having been made, some archaeologist would come and that the site would be opened, as others had been in Orkney. This was not to be, though not through lack of interest.

The truth was that the tomb was as tantalising for archaeologists. The early excavations had raised many questions and answered virtually none while, at the same time, making the potential of the site all too clear. Both the shape of the chamber and of the cairn were unusual and equally undefinable (Fig. 4), the cache of objects first found was extraordinarily rich and curiously located, and the description of some of the bones as seen was fascinating. While many Orcadian chambered tombs, excavated and unexcavated, were known to the archaeological fraternity, Isbister was the only example where one could be sure that deposits of neolithic date survived undisturbed within the chamber. The attraction of this for Colin Renfrew was great and in 1972 he took time off from his excavation of Quanterness to visit the Simisons, to walk to the cliff-edge and discuss the

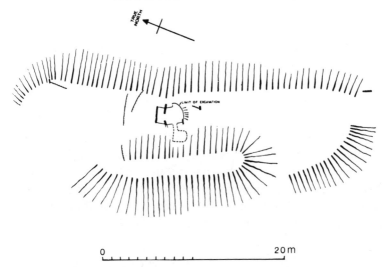

Fig. 4 Isbister, as planned in 1958; both chamber and cairn are equally incomprehensible

tomb and the work that had been done on it. The problem was not lack of interest in the site but lack of funds. The sole source of sufficient finance was the Department of the Environment and their hands were tied. There was thought to be no case for opening yet another chambered tomb to the public, nor was the site in need of being rescued from imminent destruction. Government funds were not available for purely research-based excavations and Isbister had therefore to be left as it was. Logical though this is the Simisons found it hard to accept.

Colin Renfrew's walk to the cliff-edge did, however, have its effects for on their return journey Ronald Simison took him to see a mound of burnt stones which he had been quarrying for road metalling. This proved to be a particularly fine example of one of the so-called burnt mounds which abound in Orkney and what was especially interesting about it was that the farmer said he had called a temporary halt to his quarryings when he came upon an unburnt stone building. At that time both the date and the function of these burnt mounds were somewhat enigmatic and Colin Renfrew saw that at Liddle an opportunity existed for setting the record straight. There was no shortage of volunteers from the Quanterness excavations and in one day of hectic activity a section of the mound was drawn and the building trial trenched. Rapid though it was it was the first professional work which Ronald Simison had witnessed and he was there all day, watching.

As is usually the case with such exercises very little was resolved, only potential being shown. It was particularly frustrating that no dating evidence was found. The burnt mound of Liddle, unlike the tomb of Isbister, was, however, under active threat of destruction and this permitted the funding of three seasons of work which were attached to the Quanterness project and under the immediate supervision of myself. The results of the work here, and on similar sites, were to lay the foundation for an understanding of settlement in the Bronze Age in the very north and the west of Britain. The burnt mounds turned out to be only rubbish from a peculiar method of cooking which was carried out within what were otherwise perfectly ordinary prehistoric houses. They were, moreover, the dwellings of settled agriculturalists and a programme of scientific dating showed them to belong within a period which hitherto had been a virtual blank as far as knowledge of settlements went.

All this may seem to have very little relevance to Isbister chambered tomb; in fact, it had a great deal. Ronald Simison followed every stage of the excavations at Liddle burnt mound with the keenest attention. When he had a spare moment he came and helped; in the evenings, he spent time looking at what had been done, and when any decision was made during the day or anything exciting was found he promptly appeared. This was a source of puzzlement to the group of southerners who were unacquainted with the native ability of the Orcadian to note and interpret any significant movement in an otherwise still landscape. The denim-clad farmer with the black beret was a familiar and popular figure with the diggers, appearing often with sheepdog in tow. In typical Orcadian fashion the relationship extended to the farmhouse where the frequently wet and bedraggled excavators found a ready welcome together with hot tea, food, and even warm, dry clothes. Many a pleasant evening was spent there with Ronnie and Morgan. There was no end of talk about Orkney, and of home towns further south, but the excavations at both the burnt mound and at the tomb were a recurrent theme of conversation. On the one hand, the methods and thinking used by the archaeologists were of interest; on the other there was a deep fascination with what had been found and constant speculation on what might remain.

The end of the excavations came in 1975, leaving Ronald Simison with much food for thought, but it was not the end of his connections with archaeologists. I had been overwhelmed by the attractiveness of Orkney and with the potential that existed for further work there. At the time there was no permanent archaeological presence in the Highlands and Islands and, with a certain youthful innocence, I bought and moved into the tiny stone-built dwellinghouse of Berryhill, which stood on land belonging to Lennie Scott, a nephew of the Simisons. The Simisons were now neighbours and what was already a firm friendship was extended with a great deal of advice and help being given over restoration work. It was during this period that I wrote up the results of the excavations at the burnt mound. Again, Ronald Simison was very much party to all this and followed with interest the varied work that goes on after an excavation is finished. He was familiar with the sieving and floating of samples, with specialist advice being sought and received, with radiocarbon dating, and with the ideas and objectives that lay behind the presentation of an excavated site in a published report. The publication of Liddle burnt mound appeared in 1976 and meant all the more to the Simisons because the site was on their farm. The land of their forebears could now be looked at in a perspective that went beyond the threshold of history. The Bronze Age house, left open at their request, was a source of pleasure, as was the opportunity of showing it to visitors and explaining both what had gone on there and what the surrounding land had been like at that time. Visitors were also taken to the earlier tomb at the cliff-edge but this, though of tremendous interest, made a less coherent story.

In the meanwhile I had gone on to other archaeological sites in Orkney and elsewhere in Scotland. The tomb of Isbister had once again been passed over, and for the same reason: there simply wasn't the funding available for it to be excavated professionally. A more suspicious mind might have guessed what was in the wind when Ronald Simison started to spend his evenings over Audrey Henshall's *Chambered Tombs of Scotland*. The 1,100 pages of this are far from light reading but they did constitute a storehouse of all that was then known about chambered tombs in Scotland. What was happening is quite obvious, in retrospect. Ronald Simison, already familiar with the methods and objectives of archaeological excavation, was now looking closely into what might be encountered at the cliff-edge. It was clear to him that no one else was going to excavate the tomb of Isbister within his lifetime and his solution to this personally unacceptable situation was to turn archaeologist and to do the job himself in as proper a manner as he possibly could.

Digging in earnest

There is not really a slack season for an Orkney farmer but by summer the cows have calved and the ewes have been lambed. The main preoccupation is with cutting fields left as grass, this being put down as silage to feed the livestock in the coming winter. It is a long, monotonous job which would normally have taken Ronald Simison all his time but it was one which the youngest son, Jimmy – unborn at the time of the first excavations – was more than capable of taking over. Thus released from the farmer's round Ronald had a clear two months in which to carry out his intended work. This period was not overlong but he applied himself to the task with a certain disciplined diligence. Whatever the weather he went out to the cliff-edge at nine and worked through until six, dinner being taken at the farm, midday. It was amazing what could be achieved at the hands of one person who had such determination and skill.

The first job was to take out all the earth that had been used to fill in the excavations of 1958. This had originally come from the chamber but, additionally, it was the fill of what we now know to have been an earlier excavation still. These first excavators had disturbed the human bones on the chamber floor and while some from there, and the side cell, had been taken to Edinburgh, the earth remaining was thick with fragments. No matter how small these were they were painstakingly removed by the now careful excavator of 1976. There were a lot, far too many to be put in a plastic bag or the sort of small finds tray normally found on an archaeological site, and they were fragile. The solution Ronald Simison came up with was typical of him and was one used through the rest of the excavation. One of the greatest prizes of those who search the shore around Orkney are the wooden fish-boxes which are occasionally lost at sea from trawlers. Ronald Simison had a stack of these large, stout containers at the farm and, when lined with plastic cut from fertiliser bags, they were ideal for his purpose. From the beginning everything recovered was kept safely and strictly according to the context in which it had been found.

Now, after twenty years, Ronald Simison could again look into the side cell which had caused such a stir. For Morgan it was the first time she had seen either it or the chamber it led from. The contents were now largely gone but a surprising number of bones had been left and these were duly gathered up, boxed and labelled. The careful nonchalance with which human remains were handled was very professional.

So far things had been easy; it had been largely a matter of clearing out old excavations in areas which were already familiar. The problem was what to do next. It was not an easy

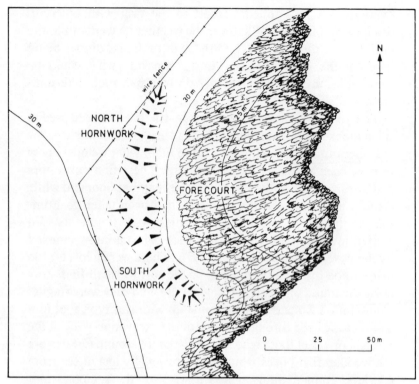

Fig. 5   Location of the site against the sheer cliffs which border the farm of Isbister

chambered tomb to tackle for, as it turned out, its shape had been seriously altered by one side being almost entirely quarried away. Not only were its contours confusing but even its extent was impossible to make out in plan. All there was on either side of what had been explored was a large elongated amorphous rise which curved rather indefinitely towards the sea (Fig. 5). Within the arms of this was a bare area of living rock, and beyond that sheer cliffs falling down to the sea. Ronald Simison was very chary of taking the Victorian expedient of following walls along within the chamber. He knew that it meant working sideways into the unknown at the risk of destroying the relationship between archaeological layers without coming to any understanding of them. Instead, he put the chamber itself to the back of his mind and decided first of all to try to work out the shape of the cairn it lay within.

The area to the immediate north of the chamber, where he had found the cache of extraordinary objects and the associated curved walling, seemed a good place to start. Having used a spade to strip a large area of turf he began trowelling away the material beneath. Next to the chamber, as was expected, he uncovered masonry and once more found the wall which he had discovered twenty years previously. This proved to be nothing less than the outer wall face of the cairn but it could plainly be seen that the surface of the mound continued on level with the surviving wall top. This was unanticipated and, more puzzling still, further trowelling showed all of this part of the rise to consist simply of loose stones with clayey earth between them. This had been put there deliberately after the tomb had been built and it was decided to remove it in order to reveal both the original ground surface and the full surviving height of the outer cairn wall (Pl. 11). As his work proceeded he encountered a few sea shells and quite a large number of bones, though the latter were not those of humans; the one exception being a solitary skull found near the base of the deposit. Of particular interest were a number of stones which he could recognise as implements, albeit crude ones (Pl. 12). At their rudest these were just beach pebbles battered through use as hammerstones but others had been fashioned to specific shapes. Among these was one which had been carefully pecked into a long point and two which were flat and rectangular with chipped parallel sides; these were later identified as being, respectively, the share from a primitive plough and probable agricultural mattock blades. In addition there were two curious implements, one about the size and shape of a table tennis bat and the other like a small, smoothed club with a short, pecked handle.

When this material to the north of the tomb had been all but removed the remains of a robbed wall 1.5 m wide was revealed along its seaward edge. This must originally have been a facing to a great bank and it could now be clearly seen, through the disparity in ground level, that this had indeed curved round towards the cliff. If the situation was the same to the south of the tomb then the hollow of bare flagstone on its seaward side must have been encompassed by such mounding and walling and would have been rather like an amphitheatre in form. Ronald Simison could not resist the temptation of removing the part of the wall immediately adjacent to the north end of the cairn. Under it, and on the foundation scarcement of the outer tomb wall, he found half of what looked like a finger ring of jet. This must have been put there between the building of the tomb and of the hornwork and went some way to giving a period for the cache of similar objects found nearby.

One feature revealed during this work not yet mentioned was a very large flat stone which was recessed into the surface of the mounding some 6 m north of the cairn. This was too large to be lifted but as the earth was removed down the side of it it was found to cover a hollow with masonry walls. This contained a skull and a number of human bones, in seeming disorder, and it was assumed that here was a cist which had been inserted at a later date into the walled bank. Later excavation showed this to have been only one of two possible explanations, though we will come to that in time.

The strange overall shape of the mound was now in part explained but the exact form of the cairn and, more particularly, the form and position of the chamber within it was as yet unclear. The solution was to open another area taking in the whole of the cairn on the seaward side of the known part of the chamber and its postulated extension southwards. This area was very much reduced in height, compared to that on the landward side, and turfing and careful cleaning revealed truncated masonry at what would have been quite a low level in the original cairn. This was, in one respect, fortunate for it made obvious the fact that the cairn was a built structure rather than just a faced pile of stones (Pl. 13, Fig. 6). Although much of the

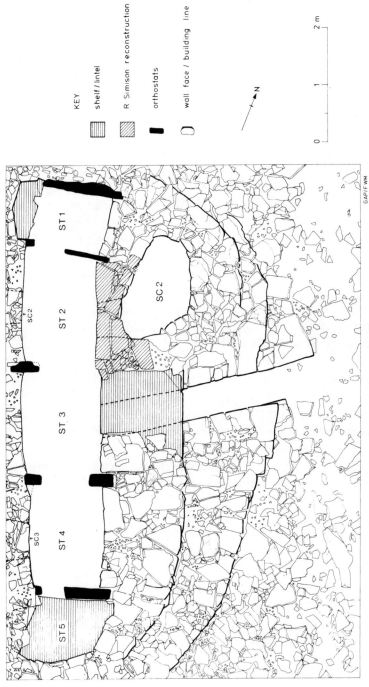

KEY

shelf / lintel

R Simison reconstruction

orthostats

wall face / building line

N

0   1   2 m

ST 1

SC 2

SC2

ST 2

ST 3

SC3

ST 4

ST 5

GAP/F WM

Fig. 6   Plan of Ronald Simison's trench over the tomb at Isbister (ST = stall; SC = side cell)

outer part was missing it could also be seen to have been built in at least two stages for there was a wall face within the body which ran parallel to what was ultimately the exterior face. In other words, the cairn when first built was smaller and was subsequently enlarged. Also revealed were another side cell, opposite that of 1958 but with its top removed, the complete length of the chamber and, coming centrally from it, the foreshortened original entrance passage to the tomb.

The plan of the central part of the monument had now been elucidated and Ronald Simison chose as his first task the excavation of the new side cell. Unlike the cell examined in 1958, this one was full of earth; removal of this filling showed that the cell had been entered before and its contents despoiled. Little remained beyond a few broken human bones. At this stage it was possible to reconstruct what had happened overall. It would seem that the site had been used as a source of building stone, possibly for buildings which are still standing. The wall which ran to the north of the cairn had been removed, work stopping as soon as the smaller stones behind it were encountered. Similarly, almost the whole of the east side of the cairn had been quarried away until the chamber was reached. Whoever the people involved were they, too, were curious at what they had found, ransacking the side cell they had broken into and digging down inside what we now know to have been the north end of the main chamber.

Only 4 m of the line of the entrance passage was preserved but the inner 1.5 m of this was still lintelled by a single massive stone. Presumably the sheer size of this prevented it being removed by the stone robbers; at the same time it was an impressive record of the skill of the people who manoeuvred it there in the first place. Beneath this the passage was filled but the material involved was sandy and completely devoid of anything of archaeological interest. These deposits looked as though they had blown in and, indeed, when they were removed, it was found that the entrance had been blocked at the inside end. What was of great interest here was that this blocking of flat, laid pieces of stone could have been done only from inside the tomb.

The whole of the top of the main chamber could now be seen and the time had come for it to be excavated. In plan it was long, extending southwards with parallel walls from the part, now empty, examined in 1958. The tips of upright stones set in the walls opposite one another gave convenient divisions to the length. These were known from similar chambers elsewhere where they partition off what are called 'stalls' – due to their similarity to the projecting stones in old-fashioned cow byres. In the case of Isbister there appeared to be five such divisions and in order to help with recording these were now numbered from the north end. The early excavation had been within stalls one and two and it was decided to excavate four and five to the south, leaving the central one for the time being in order to give a standing section of the fill.

No sooner had work started than it was found that, at the preserved height, the whole of the southernmost stall was completely taken up with a large horizontal flagstone. This was at first a puzzle but examination of the stall at the opposite end of the chamber showed this to be a shelf, its counterpart having been broken through there by the first excavators. That at the south end must have been examined, too, there being nothing much on it beyond a few bones and a blunt point made from the rib of a small whale. So far the earlier stone robbers had rather dogged Ronald Simison but it did at least look as though the fill of the fourth stall was intact and, this being the case, whatever was originally under the shelf would still be there. Though work so far had been, in some respects, disappointing, it seemed likely that this situation would now change.

The fill of the fourth stall, unlike that of those examined to the north, consisted of packed stones, most being 30 cm or less in length. To the eye of someone familiar with such materials the stones could be seen to have been laid by hand, rather than having been thrown in, and it was obvious that they were undisturbed. This material was visually the same as that which

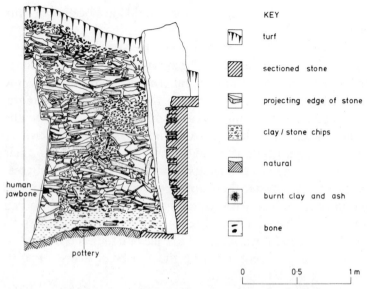

KEY

turf
sectioned stone
projecting edge of stone
clay / stone chips
natural
burnt clay and ash
bone

human
jawbone

pottery

0   0·5   1 m

Fig. 7   Section through the infill of the chamber at Isbister

Ronald Simison had seen at the inside of the blocked-up
entrance and he made the hypothesis – which proved to be
correct – that the whole chamber had been filled in from the top
by people who entered and left by the roof (Fig. 7).

Removing the fill of the fourth stall was simply a matter of
picking out the stones and occasionally removing soil and small
chips which had percolated down between them. There were
few finds to speak of, only the occasional sea shell, some
eggshell and the polished canine tooth of a dog. With depth the
shelf of the fifth stall was found to be a handy staging platform
and it was easy to work systematically and quickly. The work
was full of excitement and anticipation. After only a few layers
of stones had been removed it proved possible to look in under
the shelf – and a torch was gone for at speed. Here was the sort of
thing he had hoped for. Bare of either stones or earth, there was
a great pile of human bones – lying just as they had done when
the chamber was filled (Pl. 14).

No sooner had this exciting discovery been made than there came another. At first he found a lintel in the west wall and then, below it, the entrance into a third side cell. Though the fill of the stall it opened from had not yet been removed to floor level it was possible to peer in by the light of a torch. It was intact, unfilled, and over the whole of the floor there were human skulls lying at all angles, just as though they had been bowled in (Pl. 15). It was exactly as the first side cell discovered had been.

Ronald Simison was as yet a little off the floor of the main chamber and, as he removed what remained of the fill in the fourth stall, bones started to appear under the stones. Many were crushed, both through the weight of the fill over the centuries and, doubtless, because of the work involved in removing that fill. Operations immediately slowed down to a snail's pace with a great deal of care having to be taken in cramped conditions. The stones were gently lifted over the whole area, bones beneath being cleaned as they lay using a paintbrush, trowel and pocketknife. Such meticulous work has its rewards and, in this case, it was possible to see just how the bones had been laid on the floor, in spite of the subsequent damage that they had suffered (Pl. 16). The centre of the stall was largely bare, as though there had been access along it to the shelved stall, and, similarly, the route to the side cell entrance was clear. Elsewhere, along the sides of the stall, there were human bones in plenty and – noticeably – there were both skulls and bones belonging to other parts of the skeleton. Furthermore, it looked as though each skull had with it its own discrete pile of bones. Here was certainly a lot to think about.

As can be imagined, Ronald Simison was wild with excitement over what he had found and he soon made an appearance at the nearby cottage of Berryhill, where I was placed in an ambiguous and difficult position. On the one hand I was his friend and neighbour but on the other I was a freelance archaeologist working for the Ancient Monuments Branch of the Department of the Environment. In his desperation to see the site excavated he had formally threatened it with destruction but nevertheless the authorities were not going to like what was happening at all. I had seen Ronald Simison going across to the tomb each day but had decided against walking over to see what was happening; I did not have time to be involved deeply in a major operation and to have given advice would have meant implication. Now that I had heard how far matters had gone and what he had found I simply had to go and look for myself. From the description given the discovery sounded to be unprecedented – apart from his original find made in 1958 – and of very great importance; it was vital that, at the least, the position of the bones be verified before they were removed.

Hearing of the work was one thing but to see it was another. The scale of his operations was surprising and the skill, care, and commitment involved clearly evident. The focus of interest was, of course, the chamber. The building itself was impressive but the bones in it were an amazing sight. Those in the main chamber did indeed appear to be in heaps, each skull having with it a pile of other bones. I was interested to note that the pile of human remains under the shelf seemed lacking in skulls but the contents of the side cell made it evident where these had gone. It was clear, however, that the bones could not be left for long as they were. The site was beginning to attract visitors once more and, no matter how innocent their intentions, damage would be inevitable. It was completely impracticable with the resources and manpower at hand to plan the floor deposits and to record them in minute detail and so I decided to take photographs instead. While this was being done a colleague drew the section of the chamber fill which had been left by the excavator.

Ronald Simison now continued on his own. Generally, the bones in each of the contexts were boxed as groups. It was suspected, however, that the piles in the main chamber were somehow the remains of individuals and the clearest example was therefore kept separate so this idea could be tested. The task overall involved the lifting of literally thousands of bones

(Pl. 18), some being as small as teeth and those of the fingers and toes, and others, particularly skulls, being fragmentary. The latter left Morgan without a plastic bag in the house for it was important that all the pieces be kept together. This was slow, eerie, rather gruesome work and the excavator's dog, Butch, caused a stir one evening by coming unseen from the farm and dropping a stone down onto his master, engaged in his solitary task of cleaning round a skull. The effect was electric.

The human bones were the most obvious but mixed among them there were also those of animals and birds. Among the former Ronald Simison could identify some of sheep and cattle but it was the bird bones that aroused the strongest interest. At first he recognised talons – substantial numbers of them – and then he found a large skull which was sufficiently complete to leave no doubt of the bird in question. Astonishingly, the human and animal bones in all three contexts had those of eagles mixed among them. It was a dramatic discovery and one which was to prove to be of considerable importance.

In 1958 a few pieces of pottery and a bone bead had been recovered and the excavator had hoped to find similar objects this time. He was initially disappointed. On top of the bones under the shelf he discovered a group of twenty-one limpet shells with their apices removed which *might* have once formed a necklace but, other than two burnt lumps of struck flint which were on the floor of the fourth stall, that was all (Pl. 19).

He had now removed all the deposits from the fourth and fifth stalls and from the third side cell but one small problem remained. The fifth, shelved, stall had as its floor not the natural clay, as elsewhere, but a large flagstone which was built into its back and sides. This was higher than the floor of the main chamber but a crack showed it to be thinner than might have been expected and Ronald Simison therefore suspected that there must be a built-in gap beneath it. Prising up the fractured stone with an iron bar he found his suspicions confirmed. Beneath it was a foundation deposit of bones, some of which had belonged to eagles.

It was evident that eagles were connected with disordered human bones deposited at the time when the tomb was being built as well as when it was in use. But there was more to come. Ronald Simison was now nearing the end of his task; all that remained for him to remove was the central area of fill covering the third stall. When he was half-way down this he unexpectedly came upon a layer of human bones and with these, again, there were a large number of eagle bones, together with the remains of a crab and a couple of limpet shells. Whatever this strange method of dealing with the dead meant, and whatever the explanation for the involvement of the eagles, it was clearly a phenomenon that had lasted from the initial building of the tomb to the time when it was closed – though as yet there was no way of knowing how long that period had been.

There was about a metre of the fill to go but here too the excavator was not disappointed. The highly polished dog tooth from the fourth stall had been found close by and a bone bead had been recovered during work in 1958. Now he found twelve more beads variously fashioned from bone, shell and antler (Pl. 19). The true explanation of their presence is probably that which came most readily to mind – someone's necklace had snapped when the chamber was filled. One can almost sympathise with their vexation as they rooted between the stones looking for the lost beads.

Ronald Simison had now uncovered the inside of the massive lintel of the entrance passage and was nearing the floor. He could see the diminishing depth of fill that remained and was well prepared for the bone layer which he came upon. As in the next stall, the bones seemed to occur in piles along the sides of the wall, each having at its centre a human skull. Totally unexpected, however, and almost unbelievably there was a great mound of smashed neolithic pots along the west side of the chamber, directly opposite the now cleared entrance. This turned out to be one of the largest collections of its date ever found. There was over ½ cwt of sherds.

Ronald Simison was now well versed in the lifting of human

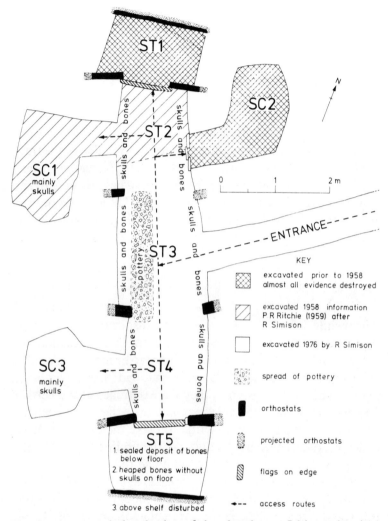

ST1

SC2

N

SC1
mainly
skulls

skulls and bones

ST2

skulls and bones

skulls and bones

skulls

0 1 2 m

ENTRANCE

skulls and bones

pottery

ST3

bones

KEY

excavated prior to 1958
almost all evidence destroyed

excavated 1958 information
P R Ritchie (1959) after
R Simison

excavated 1976 by R Simison

bones

SC3
mainly
skulls

skulls and bones

ST4

skulls and bones

spread of pottery

orthostats

projected orthostats

flags on edge

ST5
1. sealed deposit of bones
   below floor
2. heaped bones without
   skulls on floor
3. above shelf disturbed

access routes

Fig. 8 Annotated sketch-plan of the chamber at Isbister showing
contents and areas excavated (ST = stall; SC = side cell)

remains and he turned his hand with equal care to the task of
taking out all the pottery, fragment by fragment. This was quite
firm and well fired and there was little harm done in washing it.
The first I saw or heard of the collection was on being

mysteriously summoned to the farm, no explanation being given. In the kitchen at the time there was a table 8 ft long, its top taken from a wrecked ship, and it was covered from one end to the other.

The excitement was memorable, particularly as the excavations had been so successful and were now at an end (Fig. 8). But were they really finished? Ronald Simison was worried that some of the floor deposits might have contained things too small to be removed by hand and he had carefully left that in the third stall while the matter was thought over. He had seen how similar material from the burnt mound had been dealt with and saw no point in leaving the job unfinished. The next day he went to the cliff-edge with tractor and trailer, bringing home 4 cwt of earth in fertiliser bags that had been cleaned for the purpose.

A body of experts

Meanwhile I had sent a letter to the Inspectorate of Ancient Monuments in Edinburgh advising them of the situation and asking if it were at all possible for a grant to be made available, at least to record accurately the work that had been undertaken. As was only to be expected, they were outraged at the news of the excavation but, to their lasting credit, they took the situation as it was and moved swiftly to make the best of it. What had been done could not be undone, the findings were of major importance, and an account of them had to be produced while all was still fresh in the mind of the excavator. I was accordingly authorised to take over the project, though without further excavation, and to work in close collaboration with Ronald Simison; in this we were fortunate to have the skilled assistance of two other archaeologists, Sandra Øvrevik and Gordon Parry.

The first thing that had to be done was to record the structure of the tomb (Pl. 17) and its exposed outwork and surrounds. The area was surveyed generally and after the trenches had been cleaned and their sides squared they were planned. By far the trickiest problem was to delineate the chamber as this was in three dimensions but it was done as an architect would do for a standing or proposed building: plans were made at floor and shelf level and elevations were drawn of the walls together with perspective sections across the main axis (Fig. 9). A rendering of the former section across the chamber fill already existed but one had to be prepared for the material banked behind the north hornwork. In all this every stone present was accurately shown, plans being at a scale of 1:20 and sections and elevations at 1:10. In addition a comprehensive photographic record was made.

The next task was to prepare an account of the excavation work itself. This was done over several enjoyable evenings, Ronald Simison recounting his experiences and always having answers to questions on particular points. Although the stage of having a detailed site book had been dispensed with the finished result was quite creditable, it proving possible to draft such a statement as would be the outcome of an archaeological excavation conducted under more usual circumstances. The excavator had this to mull over for a while and, after a few alterations, clarifications and additional points had been made, the account was adopted and was published more or less verbatim under joint authorship in the final report on the site.

The third necessary stage of recording was to prepare a catalogue of all the finds that had been made. Not only was it important to ensure that the original context of everything had been put down but all the artefacts and samples had to be cleaned and clearly marked. The fish-boxes of bones were now stacked high in an outhouse, their ends painted white and bearing such curious codes as IS'76 BC 6; ST 5, L3. Similarly, even the beads were marked with numbers which identified them with the site and the spot where they were found.

We were not yet finished with all the finds and samples. Bones were taken for radiocarbon analysis, two from each context, and wrapped securely in several layers of dense plastic. The pottery was examined for hour upon hour, any sherds that fitted being glued together. Morgan was the chief operative here

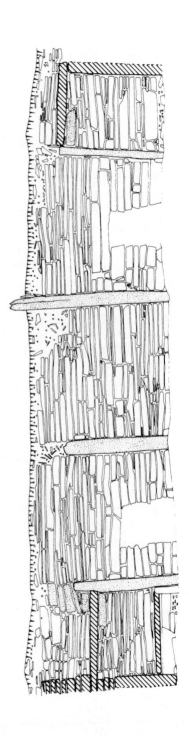

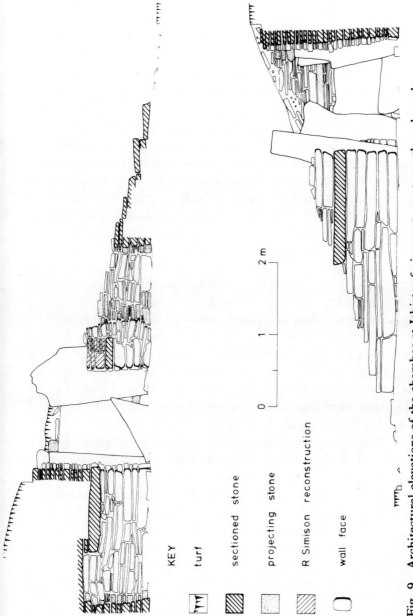

KEY

turf

sectioned stone

projecting stone

R Simison reconstruction

wall face

0   1   2 m

Fig. 9   Architectural elevations of the chamber at Isbister facing east, west, north and south

having trays of sand in which to rest the setting joins and gaining great satisfaction from seeing the broken vessels take shape once more. In the meantime the earth Ronnie had taken from the chamber floor was gently drying under a heat-radiating lamp designed originally to keep litters of piglets warm. Once it was dry he stirred it batch by batch into water in a large bin, more normally used for brewing the household beer. Mud is un-inspiring at the best of times but to everyone's delight carbon floated off, some of the pieces being readily identified as barley grains. After some experimentation he found that the best method of recovery was to use a saucer to skim with, just as the cream was taken from the settled milk of the family milch cow; this was, admittedly, used in conjunction with a 200 micron sieve. The mud was then hosed through a 5 mm sieve where, again, another pleasant surprise was in store, for among the millions of small stones in the residue were mixed thousands of fish-bones. Sorting these tiny remains out with a camel hair brush and tweezers proved to be quite the most time-consuming aspect of the whole operation but everyone took a turn and some 6,500 fragments were recovered. This sieving proved beyond doubt how effective the hand collection of objects had been. In the residue there were almost exclusively unidentifiable small fragments of human and other bone – though there were also one or two burnt flints and fragments of at least three little bone pins, which were similarly calcined.

We were very fortunate in then obtaining the help of a number of prominent specialists – a veritable body of experts. The various finds from the tomb were sent off, by one means or another, and there then followed a long wait while information and results trickled back.

The human bones formed the bulk of the material and we were particularly lucky to secure the services of Judson T. Chesterman, an authority with many demands on his time. Mr Chesterman, a retired surgeon, works from the Department of Prehistory and Archaeology at the University of Sheffield where he specialises in what can only be described as the intensive analysis of human remains. He had dealt with large collections before and, as one of these had been the bones from Quanterness chambered tomb, we simply could not have found anyone more suitable. The bones from the 1976 excavations were accordingly crated in tea-chests and sent by carrier. On their arrival Chesterman sorted out all the animal and bird remains and then set methodically about the massive task before him. In addition, the bones removed to Edinburgh in 1958 were located and reunited with the others of the collection. In all there were a staggering 16,000 bones and fragments and the analysis, started in January 1978, was to occupy Chesterman almost full time until June 1981. I took the opportunity of visiting Chesterman while he worked and found him to be a colourful and very likeable character. Working in a surgeon's smock among tables of bones he pointed out traces of illnesses, deformities, and inherited characteristics with an enthusiasm which was infectious. Mr Chesterman obviously loved his work and the results of his labour – as distilled from books of notes – proved to be very worthwhile indeed. Sheffield is a noted centre for the teaching and practice of all branches of medicine and Chesterman was able to discuss and confirm his findings with authorities on particular aspects. His work is a model of research, with almost every avenue explored.

I say 'almost' with reason for this unparalleled collection of early bones has attracted subsequent interest. At an early stage of my university career I had studied demography and saw an opportunity here of applying the methods of this subject to such a large, well-analysed collection of human remains from the past. It was a chance that it would have been ridiculous to have passed over and, though Chesterman was, and remains, sceptical, I believe the results to be an important step towards understanding the structure and dynamics of an early population. Mr Chesterman was similarly disenchanted with the approach of Elizabeth Glenn of Ball State University, Indiana. For some time she had studied such human skulls of neolithic and Bronze Age date as had been found in Britain and was so impressed with the quality and quantity of the remains from Isbister that she has used them as the focus of a computer analysis based on measurement. This gives insight into what might be called racial characteristics over time and space and, though her paper is in the process of being published, Elizabeth Glenn has given permission for it to be previewed in this book. A third approach, taken by Professor G.E. Bacon of the Department of Physics of Sheffield University, is the study of stress distribution in bones by neutron diffraction. It is hoped that this will further some of Chesterman's conclusions regarding the unusual musculature of the legs of the people of Isbister but, unfortunately, the results are not yet to hand. There is certainly enough said here on the subject of the human bones, but it gives an idea of the type of information that will be presented later.

The environmental remains were put in similarly expert hands. Mr Chesterman passed about 1,000 animal bones and fragments to his colleague Graeme Barker whose analysis is equally thorough and far-reaching in its conclusions. More than 700 bird bones were sent to Don Bramwell in Derbyshire; he had reported on those from Quanterness and consented to look at the Isbister samples before retiring for good. His ability to identify even the tiniest piece leaves one in wonder but, in this respect, the work of Sarah Colley at Southampton University is perhaps even more remarkable. Miss Colley specialises in 'marine resource remains' and this included not just the crab shells, sea shells, and the single piece of a whale, but also all the fish bones that had been recovered. Through using the comparative collections of both the Southampton Faunal Remains Project and the Natural History Museum in London she was able to identify no less than 2,500 of these. A similarly unenviable job fell to Sheila Sutherland, then at Sheffield; she had all the tiny animal bones and 1,200 of these were variously attributed to frogs, voles and mice. Finally, more than 300 carbonised seeds were examined by Ann Lynch, then studying at one of the best possible places for the subject, the Instituut voor Prae en Proto-historie in Amsterdam. Though there were environmental remains, no samples relating broadly to the overall landscape had been recovered during the excavation. Ronald Simison had, however, found pieces of small trees and even hazel nuts while draining a piece of land near Liddle farmhouse and it was obvious that the waterlogged peat deposit these came from related to the neolithic period, if not before. Work on this was outside my remit but, luckily, a geographer from Kingston Polytechnic, Darius Bartlett, came to me for advice on choosing a location for pollen analysis. A marriage of interests was arranged and I got a superb record of the overall environment of the area in neolithic times, linking with the work done for the Bronze Age burnt mound, while his resultant undergraduate dissertation led him on to postgraduate research at Edinburgh University.

The radiocarbon samples, too, received the best attention. As has been mentioned, two were taken from each context and, where possible, sub-samples of each of these were sent for analysis at laboratories in both Glasgow and Cambridge. This permitted Michael Stenhouse and Roy Switsur, respectively, to check their results against those of the other and it gave a series of dates which were as faultless as possible. The overall supervision of the radiocarbon dating programme, and the responsibility of synthesising and interpreting the results, rested with Colin Renfrew.

Finally, there were the artefacts: the pottery and the other small finds that had been recovered. These included the ones which had been found in 1958 and which were retrieved from the National Museum of Antiquities, where they had been exhibited on loan. There could be no better person to look at all of these than Audrey Henshall and, arrangements having been made, the Simisons took the objects, in person, to her in Edinburgh. She, in turn, sought the advice of other experts. Samples were taken of all the pots, using a saw and pliers, and were submitted to David Williams of Southampton University for thin section analysis of the clay from which they were made.

Dr A.S. Clarke and G.H. Collins of the Royal Scottish Museum identified the sources of the materials from which the other artefacts had been fashioned and Caroline Wickham-Jones of the National Museum of Antiquities of Scotland Artifact Research Unit deliberated on the curious stone knife found in 1958.

While specialist work is in progress the publication of a site report is more or less in limbo and during this period I was heavily engaged on the large, multi-period excavation at Howe near Stromness. Some weekends and evenings were, however, spent in South Ronaldsay and talk of Isbister continued, fired by the periodic arrival of reports on material sent away. Obviously, problems remained which could be resolved only by excavation and at this stage Ronald Simison, rather unexpectedly, put a long trench into the north hornwork around the edge of the central tomb structure. Mercifully, no finds were made but he did prove that the outer tomb wall had been built with a sheer face and that this and the material against it survived to a height of almost 2 m. This was very interesting information, adding greatly to our knowledge of the third, vertical, dimension of the monument as a whole. It was also interesting that the outer tomb wall had been in danger of collapse at one point and had been propped with rough masonry between the time it was built and the time it was covered with the stones and clay of the hornwork. The reaction of the Inspectorate of Ancient Monuments to this revival of work can be imagined but, having made their displeasure clear, a small grant for recording was made and Stephen Carter and Kay Darbyshire were seconded from the Howe excavations.

This was a relatively small interlude in what seemed to be an endless wait for the last of the specialist work to be finished. In preparation for this time the line illustrations for the academic report on the site had been drawn up by Frank Moran of the North of Scotland Archaeological Services and with the eventual arrival of Chesterman's script the way was clear for writing to begin. The composition of the resulting book took a year, from the summer of 1981 to the summer of 1982. By this time I had moved down to Beaconsfield in Buckinghamshire where the peace and solitude of a garden summerhouse was complemented by the accessibility of the London libraries.

I may well have been responsible for the publication but the work it rested on was that of a team and I decided that it should be presented as such. As mentioned, the description of the excavation was that given to me by Ronald Simison, and the various specialist reports, instead of being put as appendices, were remodelled so as to make separate chapters within a coherent text. My individual contribution was to write the last four of thirteen chapters. Here Isbister found a place in the history of tomb exploration in Orkney; its structure and use was compared to that of others; and the people, their environment, culture and society were discussed at length. In doing this I became aware of just how great the contribution of Isbister was to our understanding of the neolithic period in Orkney, and elsewhere. The site had attracted the attention of the media and the interest of the public and the whole matter was worthy of the sort of wider readership that could be reached only through a broadly based and less technically written work.

Tomb of the Eagles was a long way off and just as the manuscript of its academic counterpart was in the final stages of production news came through that Ronald Simison had started work again. This time the Inspectorate of Ancient Monuments came down heavily, threatening legal action under the stringent Ancient Monuments Act which had just been passed by Parliament. By the time the letter arrived, however, Ronald Simison had solved all the problems he sought answers to and he has rested content since. He had a series of trenches which showed several points (Fig. 10). First, the outline of the original tomb had not been round, as had previously been projected, but oval, and it could now be seen to be preserved, on the west, to the astonishing height of almost 3 m where, moreover, the top was curving inwards. Second, he found that the south end of the tomb was recessed into the ground and that the rise of the

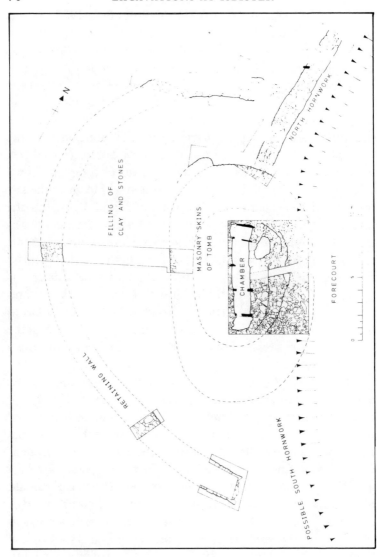

Fig. 10   Areas excavated at Isbister up to 1982

'southern hornwork' was a natural one which had been taken advantage of, being artificially complemented to the north. Thirdly, he discovered that the supposed cist in the north hornwork was actually a cavity in a built wall which went right round the back of the tomb on top of half a metre of stones and clay. As radiocarbon dating had shown the contents of this 'cist' to be much later than even the closure of the chamber this opened the possibility that the monument as a whole had been under construction and in use for a very long period indeed with the upper part of the banking material being late. A record of this work was made by David Haigh and Stephen Carter, from the still continuing Howe excavations, and, the site having been visited by me, an appendix was added to the report in press.

Questions do remain which could be answered, particularly through more formal excavation, but, as far as we know, no further work will be carried out at Isbister in the foreseeable future. The work that has been done is more exhaustive and informative than that on any similar site and now, with the excavation behind us, we move on to an appreciation of the impact that Isbister has had on our insight into a strange and exciting part of our collective past.

3 · Tombs for Tribesmen

The building of Isbister tomb

It was James Fergusson who first appreciated that structures such as that at Isbister were architecture in a sophisticated sense. This is not necessarily to say that they were designed and built by architects and master masons but that they are part of a distinctive tradition of form and that their construction involved a great deal of skill and an intimate appreciation of the qualities of the main material used. This is the first point. The second is that, as Isbister goes to show, such structures were not designed and erected at one time but were the product of generations of involvement and building; in this sense they are rather like our cathedrals. The tombs were, in several ways, a dominant part of the culture of the people who built and used them and in this chapter and the following we will be exploring this together with such matters as the reasons directing their siting, their implications for the structure of society, and the duration of their term. First of all, however, we will look into the process by which Isbister itself was built and will then compare its structure with that of the other excavated tombs of Orkney.

The masonry we know of at Isbister was not completely removed by the excavator and we cannot and must not suppose that it necessarily represents the total span of use of the site. The monument we see now may have been gradually built up on an area which had been the centre of yet earlier activity. The foundation deposit does indeed point to this; it is unlikely that the human bones involved were brought from very far afield because the bird remains with them were from white-tailed sea eagles, which have a preference for a habitat with cliffs (or trees). The possibility of a less grand form of ossuary than a chambered tomb is not mere supposition for a simple cist recently found on Sumburgh Airport in Shetland contained the disordered bones of at least eighteen individuals and was dated to the earliest part of the neolithic period.

Radiocarbon dating of the bones of the Isbister foundation deposit did not show them to be discernibly earlier than some in the chamber. This is, perhaps, disappointing but it does permit us to pinpoint the start of the building of the tomb with an unusual exactness (Fig. 11) to 3150 (± 80) BC.

The first job to be done was to level the site for the tomb itself; it is likely that even at this stage it was conceived as being part of a larger area of use, as it was placed centrally against the frontage of bare flagstones and fitted into the natural bank which in part surrounded this. The reduction of the ground-level at what was to be the south end of the chamber must have been achieved with such primitive instruments as pointed digging sticks, the shoulder blades of cattle, antlers used as picks and, possibly, mattocks of stone such as those found in the excavations; there were no spades, shovels, or pickaxes as we know them. The internal plan of the chamber must also have been laid out according to a predetermined design. As will be seen the plans of chambers vary in systematic ways and while the reasoning behind this has not yet been fathomed the fairly obvious point must be made that once a design had been implemented there were only very limited ways in which the chamber could be expanded or otherwise altered. Whatever their reasons, the people at Isbister marked out a chamber with three central stalls, two end ones – which were to be shelved – an entrance opening from the side, and three side cells. There was deliberation in this as well as design; it was, for example, quite intentional that there were to be three side cells instead of a more symmetrical four.

The long upright slabs had now to be quarried for the divisions between the stalls and these, and the other stone involved, would almost certainly have been taken from the area

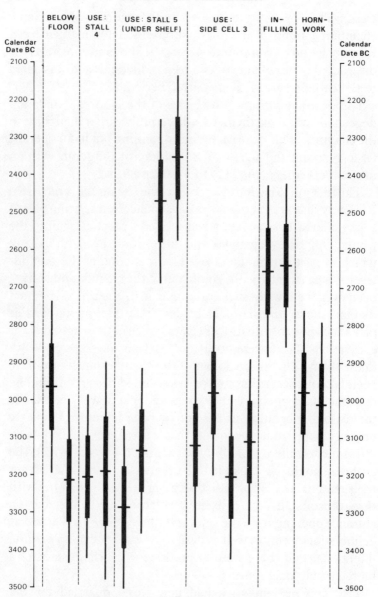

Fig. 11 Calibrated radiocarbon dates for Isbister. Note: those for bones from the 'megalithic' cist are not shown

in front of what was to be the tomb. The effect of deepening what was already a natural shallow depression may well have been desired. The stone there is hard but, like Orkney sandstone generally, it is laminated and easily split. This would probably have been achieved using wooden wedges while such shaping as was deemed necessary could have been effected with hammerstones brought from the beach. Even the largest of the uprights could have been carried, or dragged, using ropes of hide or, conceivably, of twisted straw and they would have been quite easily levered into a prepared socket and propped temporarily in position.

The general standard of stonework at Isbister, and elsewhere, is of such a quality that it must have been done by skilled hands and it is reasonable to imagine a certain division of labour between quarrying, carrying, and the actual process of building. The sandstone involved splits with flat, straight edges and these would have been used to face both the interior and exterior of the rising tomb; between these two faces other stones were laid in a close fitting mosaic. The horizontal section provided by the trench over the chamber and the cairn to the east of it showed how carefully this had been done with the exposed side cell being taken account of and with the wall varying in overall width from 1 m to 3 m in order to give the whole structure an oval rather than a rectangular basal plan.

Building was, however, far from a matter of just erecting a vertical wall. The false floors of the two end stalls had to be inserted at an early stage and these areas were later shelved using projecting stones built into the walls for supports. Around this time the massive stone which lintelled the inner part of the entrance passage must have been dragged into place, probably with the use of a specially built ramp and rollers. There is a great deal of sophistication here and this can also be traced in the interior walls of the chamber. The stones here are flush, probably banged into final position with hammerstones, but they are also set in a horizontal bow between uprights. This would have acted in the same way as a Roman, Norman, or later stone arch, spreading the pressure from the cairn behind and locking all the masonry into place. While the walls were being built the circuits of masonry around the side cells were gradually diminished in circumference until these could be ceiled with a single stone. This is the corbelling effect previously mentioned and this technique can also now be seen in the main chamber and in the end stalls. In the latter the wall above the shelves was built out so as to form pillars which went up to the roof while their backs were corbelled in. Similarly the walls of stalls two to four were brought gradually in, making a great pointed arch which would have been capped at a height approaching 3 m.

This, then, was the gloomy interior of the tomb as first built (Fig. 12). From the outside it would have been a prominent grey, oval-shaped dome, measuring some 10 m by 8 m and having an outer face which was nearly vertical for 3 m and then curved in to the maximum height of some 3.5 m. Even this first stage represented a prodigious effort involving as it did more than 200 cu m of masonry.

The tomb was then put into use but within the next few generations the builders added an outer casing of masonry which was almost 2 m wide at the sides and some 4 m thick at the ends. This again gave a structure with an almost vertical outer wall face but one which was more of an elongated oval in basal plan and which measured 18 m by 11 m. In doing this stone was quarried for an additional 300 cu m of masonry.

Sufficient time then elapsed for part of the west side of the outer tomb wall to start to collapse; it had to be shored with a rough buttress of stone. The next stage of construction occurred around 2995 (± 80) BC. This involved the building of the wall which went from the foundation footing of the tomb northwards, curving round the edge of the frontage of bare flagstone, towards the sea. It will be remembered that this was found to

Fig. 12   An artist's reconstructed view of the interior of the chamber at Isbister (*Alex Rigg*)

cover half of a jet ring. The wall having been built, a mixture of clay and stones was dumped behind it in order to match the natural rise to the south. Animal bones found at the bottom provided the date for this phase of activity.

How high the wall was and how much material was dumped behind it at any one time is a problem, as phasing now becomes a little uncertain. It is certain, however, that at first the depth of the latter material did not exceed 0.5 m, for built on it at this height was another, and similar, wall which went round the back of the tomb giving it a semicircular shape. This wall may belong to the period around 3000 BC or, alternatively, it may have been built around 1595 (± 110) BC. It all depends on whether the human bones found in it were contemporary or whether they had been subsequently inserted into its structure. In either case the next stage of building was to dump more stones and clay both on the inside and on the outside of the semicircular wall, this material rising to a known surviving height of almost 3 m against the west side of the outer tomb wall. There is little reason why this should later have been removed and the likelihood is that it tailed off in all directions and that the semicircular wall was never much more than 1 m high. It can be conjectured, therefore, that at one time or another the front wall of the hornwork was 2–3 m high next to the tomb and that its top would then have sloped rapidly down to the height of the wall which was butted at right angles to it. It seems only reasonable that this façade was mirrored by another to the south of the tomb, though all trace of it now seems to have been removed. It is a little difficult to calculate the volume of material used in this third stage of construction, taking it all together, but figures of 125 cu m for the stone and 300 cu m for the dumped material would seem reasonable.

But what of the closure of the tomb? In order to date this bones were selected from those in the fill though in the event one sample consisting of eagle bones was considered too precious to use. The other sample gave dates which averaged out at 2650 (± 80) BC but, curiously, a bone referable to the use of the chamber proved to be later still. The only reasonable explanation of this is that human bones of some antiquity had been incorporated in the fill. Taking one consideration with the other Colin Renfrew postulated that the infilling of the chamber had not taken place until around 2400 BC. This means that the tomb had been open for some 800 (± 180) years, which is a phenomenal period of time. It is very interesting indeed, however, that five of the six samples involved suggested that the chamber had been used intensively as an ossuary only for the first 160 years of this (or, at most, 320, with 68 per cent certainty). This, notwithstanding, it can be seen from the later bone in the chamber spoken of and those in the fill that the practice of depositing eagles with disordered human remains continued for the 800 years and, even more amazingly, the bones in the 'cist' in the hornwork prove that both the site and at least the basic element of a bizarre burial ritual were still used around 1600 BC. This period stretches over more than one and a half thousand years – the timespan that stands between us and the fall of the Roman empire.

To return to the monument itself, it can be seen that a very good picture of what it looked like at each stage of its construction can be obtained. In its final form it must have been a magnificent sight and a very important feature, as previously, was its great forecourt of flagstone. The amount of effort that went into building the structure was phenomenal, more than 900 cu m of material being involved; it takes little imagination to appreciate the significance that it must have had for the generations that laboured over its erection, let alone those that followed. To know of one such monument belonging to so remote a period of antiquity is remarkable enough but the fact is that no less than seventy-six are known in Orkney as a whole – of which Isbister must be accounted among the most splendid.

Other Orcadian tombs

The best-documented aspect of the Orcadian tombs is their structure and, above all, the form of their chambers. This is a consequence of the way in which information has been accumulated, being mostly the product of unsophisticated excavation coupled with very good non-exploratory fieldwork. The main contribution of the Victorians, as ultimately seen in the work of Joseph Anderson, was classification backed by an awareness of date and it must be said that the typological foundation laid then has withstood the test of time, being clearly discernible in the later groupings of Gordon Childe, Stuart Piggott and Audrey Henshall. Since then a very good computer analysis has been effected by David Fraser but at this point it is easier to describe the chambers under the headings given by Henshall since the results of Fraser's work support rather than disagree with these.

In *Maes Howe type* tombs a passage leads to a square or rectangular chamber from which there is access to a number of side cells. Only seven definite examples of this form are known: on Mainland there is Maes Howe itself, Cuween, Wideford Hill and Quanterness; while in the North Isles there is a curious specimen on the Holm of Papa Westray; and two more normal ones, Vinquoy Hill on Eday and Quoyness on Sanday. The numbers have been, perhaps dubiously, swelled by the addition of a further five examples on the basis of old and vague records or a supposed connection of the type with carved stones. Even disregarding these it remains certain that many more chambers of the type must have existed; the problem is that they are impossible to identify without excavation.

In the *tripartite chambers* there is a pair of portal stones at the inside of the entrance passage and the chamber itself is divided into three lineally related sections by pairs of similar stones projecting from the side walls; the back wall is generally formed of one stone. The *stalled chambers* are simply an extension of this idea whereby the chamber is elongated and the number of paired divisions increased; sometimes these are entered from the side. It must be pointed out that a chamber incorporated into the Calf of Eday Long has only two stalls and, therefore, fits neither category. A note of caution should preface a list of tripartite and stalled chambers for while the characteristic line of paired orthostats makes for easy identification when a cairn has been eroded or mutilated, the example of Isbister shows us that the chamber may have additional features which are not visible and which would be unusual for this type. Six tombs with tripartite chambers have been excavated: Huntersquoy (upper chamber) and Sandyhill Smithy on Eday; and Bigland Round, Kierfea Hill, the Knowe of Craie and the slightly aberrant site of the Knowe of Lairo on Rousay. Similarly, strictly speaking, there are only seven certain examples of stalled chambers: Blackhammer, Knowe of Ramsay, Knowe of Rowiegar, Knowe of Yarso and Midhowe on Rousay; one on the north end of the Holm of Papa Westray; and another on the Calf of Eday. There are certainly many other sites which have stalls.

Henshall's fourth chamber form is the *Bookan type*. The chambers are sub-circular in plan and have radial divisions projecting from their walls resulting in a central space – which is virtually a continuation of the passage – surrounded by compartments. These compartments are divided off by benches, or orthostats, with gaps between, or low kerbs. In addition to the type site of Bookan on Mainland, there are two examples on the Calf of Eday, the lower compartment at Huntersquoy, Eday, and both the upper and lower compartments at Taversoe Tuick on Rousay. It should be noted that all except Bookan were partly subterranean. There can be little doubt that the otherwise anomalous rock-cut tomb on Hoy, the Dwarfie Stane, has a floor plan which has most in common with the Bookan type tombs.

When Henshall came to the excavated site of Unstan, which has five stalls and a side cell, she listed it simply as having a stalled chamber on the grounds that, although their occurrence is very rare, side cells are found in similar chambers in the north of mainland Scotland. Isbister had then only been partially examined and the same judgement was passed on the side cell found there together with a conjectured one at a poorly recorded site on Burray. Now that the chamber at Isbister has been fully excavated we are forced to look at the situation anew. In addition to five stalls it has no less than three side cells and these, together with the one at Unstan, have a great deal more in common with the side cells found in the Maes Howe group than with those few odd examples discovered on the other side of the Pentland Firth. It looks very much as though the chambers at Isbister and Unstan should be regarded as a hybrid type which incorporates distinctive features of both the stalled and Maes Howe varieties. If we take into consideration only the chambers whose shapes are certain then this hybrid, as a fifth group, makes up some 7 per cent of the sample.

Just a glance at the accompanying plans of the tombs (Fig. 13) shows that the chambers, of whatever type, vary considerably in size. Some are tiny with a floor area of only 5 sq m while in the case of the largest, the Holm of Papa Westray South, the total extent of the interior is more than eleven times greater than this. The majority of the chambers known are on the small side, half having an area of less than 11 sq m and that of Isbister could scarcely be thought of as grand at 13 sq m. It can also be seen that within each type the architectural tradition and the properties of the stone used dictated the form which larger chambers had to take. Under normal circumstances a central chamber could not be much more than 2 m wide because it would otherwise be impossible to give it a roof at a reasonable height through corbelling. That Maes Howe is an exception is well worth noting but usually a larger floor area could be achieved only by lengthening the chamber and, in the case of Maes Howe and hybrid types, by increasing the number of side cells. Extreme examples of this are seen at the Knowe of Ramsay and the Holm of Papa Westray South, these having, respectively, fourteen stalls and fourteen side cells. Neither arrangement was possible in the case of the Bookan type chambers and it is conceivable that Taversoe Tuick and

Huntersquoy were built originally with two storeys for this reason.

Because of the way the chambers were built an increase in size was directly equivalent to an increase in the number of compartments whether stalls or side cells. This complicates matters for it may well be that what was desired in planning a tomb was a certain arrangement of compartments, the size of the chamber necessitated by this being incidental. Rather than simply wondering why some chambers are larger than others it is necessary to question why some people required sepulchres with more compartments than others and to consider what the significance might be of the different types of compartments.

Isbister has taught us that different types of compartment *were* used for different purposes but it and Unstan are anomalous in having three kinds: there are stalls, the shelved end recesses, and side cells.

In the other forms of chamber there are only two, tripartite and stalled ones having stalls and end compartments, the Maes Howe types having a central chamber and side cells, and the Bookan type having a central area and peripheral divisions. Isbister has also shown us that chambers were further divided by necessary routes of access so that each stall may be thought of as being in two halves and the central chamber and area of Maes Howe and Bookan tombs may similarly be considered to have been partitioned by pathways. The problem of variability in the number of compartments and other complexities still remains. Why were tripartite chambers built with two stalls and an end compartment while the stalled chambers had as many as thirteen stalls to only one compartment of the second type? Similarly, why do the number of side cells in Maes Howe type tombs vary from three to as many as fourteen? Interesting complexities include the fact that Isbister, Unstan, and Blackhammer were entered from the side and have therefore two rather than one end compartment, that the first two of these sites additionally have side cells, and that at Cuween Hill and the Holm of Papa Westray South some of the side cells are in

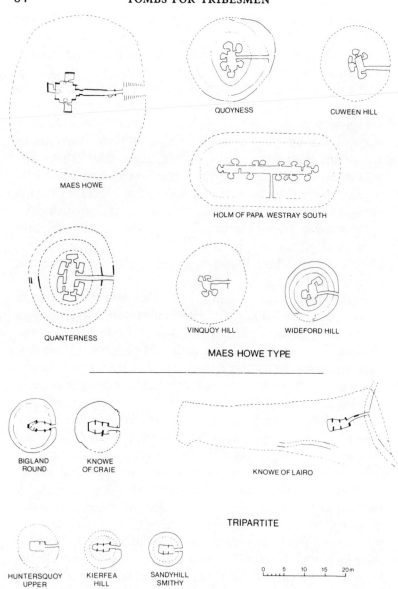

QUOYNESS

CUWEEN HILL

MAES HOWE

HOLM OF PAPA WESTRAY SOUTH

QUANTERNESS

VINQUOY HILL

WIDEFORD HILL

MAES HOWE TYPE

BIGLAND
ROUND

KNOWE
OF CRAIE

KNOWE OF LAIRO

TRIPARTITE

HUNTERSQUOY
UPPER

KIERFEA
HILL

SANDYHILL
SMITHY

0   5   10   15   20 m

Fig. 13 Types of tomb chambers found in Orkney (*after A.S. Henshall*)

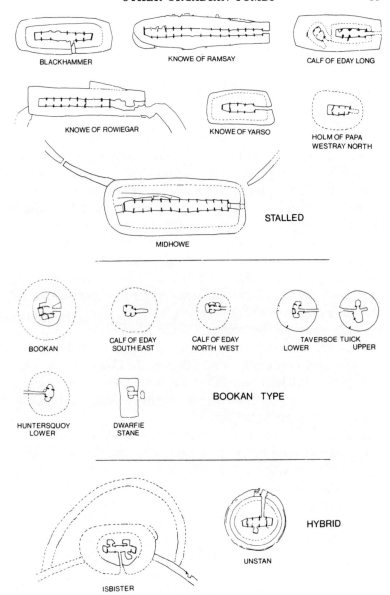

BLACKHAMMER

KNOWE OF RAMSAY

CALF OF EDAY LONG

KNOWE OF ROWIEGAR

KNOWE OF YARSO

HOLM OF PAPA
WESTRAY NORTH

STALLED

MIDHOWE

BOOKAN

CALF OF EDAY
SOUTH EAST

CALF OF EDAY
NORTH WEST

TAVERSOE TUICK
LOWER   UPPER

HUNTERSQUOY
LOWER

DWARFIE
STANE

BOOKAN TYPE

HYBRID

UNSTAN

ISBISTER

two distinct parts, though sharing a common entrance.

With the level of information available the meaning of all this can only be guessed at, though Isbister has taken us a little way further. The likelihood is that the differences in compartment types within a chamber are connected with stages of funerary ritual but that the numbers of each type, and the proportion of one to the other, is in some way connected with the structure of the groups which used the tombs. It is not impossible that fresh and exacting excavations will help elucidate this for, as Chesterman's analysis of the Isbister bones shows, genetic relationships can be traced in certain instances. If this guess is correct then the chambers now seen must relate to the social structure of the builders when the monuments were first erected, whatever local changes occurred in social structure thereafter. As has been mentioned, it would have been very difficult to have brought about a change in chamber plan once a design had been implemented. This *may* be an alternative explanation of the second storeys at Huntersquoy and Taversoe Tuick and, certainly, lines in the masonry at the Knowe of Rowiegar do suggest that four stalls were added there. The clearest instance of a chamber becoming outmoded is at the Calf of Eday Long where one tomb with two stalled compartments was supplanted by another with four and it may be that more tombs were rebuilt than is commonly supposed.

One fact about the dynamic aspect of tomb building that can be stated with more certainty is that tombs once built were often increased in outward size. Although they have only rarely been purposely and exhaustively looked for, the sort of internal masonry line seen at Isbister is a common occurrence in cairns covering all types of chamber. Sometimes these have been observed in plan and at other times mention is made of vertical lines in the masonry of passages. For some tombs there is no information but known examples indicate that the innermost skin of the cairn generally consisted of a wall 1.5–2.5 m thick and that subsequent skins were of similar width. Other things being equal the overall size of the cairn would therefore have been proportional at each stage to that of the internal chamber. The option was, however, not always taken up and while Quanterness had no less than three skins the Knowe of Rowiegar and the Knowe of Ramsay are known to have had only one – though in both of these cases there is an adherent lump of masonry of appropriate thickness that may have been the start of an intended enlargement.

The size of the cairns involved varies enormously – the smallest, the Calf of Eday NW, covering an area of only 50 sq m while Maes Howe and the enigmatic Earl's Knoll on Papa Stronsay are twenty times that size. Most are on the small side, with areas up to 250 sq m but there are a significant number of larger ones and it is interesting that Isbister can be included among the latter only on account of the third phase of construction, that connected with the hornworks. Shapes are variable and while the majority tend to be round in plan a number are more rectangular and this, not surprisingly, includes those with especially long chambers. There are also some curious shapes, the Knowe of Lairo on Rousay and the Head of Work near Kirkwall being unusual in having the chamber at one end of a long body of material and the cairn of Burray, seemingly, being almost square but for two opposing concave sides. The volumes of stonework and other material involved will be discussed at a later stage but mention should be made here of one or two interesting conclusions which David Fraser came to in the course of his analysis. He found that variation in chamber size was nowhere near as marked as variation in cairn size. It might be expected that the larger chambers had larger cairns, but he discovered that there was little connection; a relatively large chamber might be contained within a relatively small cairn and vice versa. Further, there was no obvious correlation between the final shape of the cairn and the original form of the chamber. It seems that we are observing not just a dynamic process but one which varied. A tomb having been built by one group it may have been enlarged to a varying degree or left unaltered according to the desires, resources, and ability of their descendants, the final shape being in part dictated by ideas prevalent at the time of the last stage of building. It might be reasonable to interpret the difference in size of the chambers and that of the cairns that ultimately surrounded them as reflecting the waxing or waning fortunes of the groups involved. But, as will be seen, the implications may be deeper; the changing structure of society itself may be involved.

Plans are one thing but it will be remembered that in the case of Isbister it was possible to obtain a fairly good idea of what the tomb looked like when it was intact. Evidence from other sites suggests that the view obtained may be generalised with confidence, though obvious exceptions are the two known double-decker tombs and those which were subterranean. These anomalous examples are all rather small and were roofed by slabbing at a height of between 1–2 m but it is likely that most, if not all, of the other chambers were corbelled. This suggests that they, and their surrounding cairns, must therefore have been quite high and this is substantiated by figures for the well-preserved chambers of Quoyness, Knowe of Lairo and Maes Howe which range from 4 m to 4.5 m. The chamber of the Holm of Papa Westray S became dilapidated between its excavation in 1849 and its being placed under guardianship in 1929 but it is known that its walls were originally preserved to a height of about 3 m and that they overhung to within 80 cm of each other. Further, while the outermost wall at Quoyness survived only to a height of just over 1 m the two internal lines – which are assumed to be outer walls in their turn – were around 3 m high. The evidence from here, and elsewhere, supports the idea given by Isbister that the outer wall faces of the tombs were almost vertical. This seems reasonable and possible in the case of the majority of the tombs since they were stone built throughout but Maes Howe and the example recently discovered under Iron Age settlement at the Howe, Stromness, are unusual in that the 'cairn' is of clay; here, too, however, there are outer revetments of stone. That such outer wall faces were intended to be seen as part of the visible architecture of the structure as a whole is

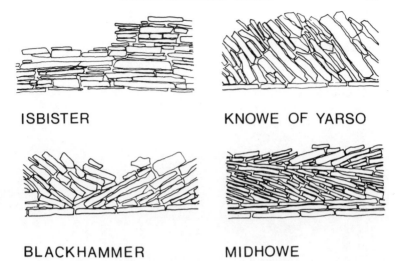

ISBISTER   KNOWE OF YARSO

BLACKHAMMER   MIDHOWE

Fig. 14   Patterns of stonework on external tomb walls (*after D. Fraser*)

clearly indicated by the designs worked in them at the Knowe of Yarso, Blackhammer and Midhowe (Fig. 14).

At Isbister there is a magnificent forecourt but in looking for such areas elsewhere there are the problems that they may have existed without being formally defined, that any structures involved will have been especially liable to damage, and that even the immediate surroundings of tombs have hardly been investigated at all. In spite of this a number of parallels may be cited. Both the Knowe of Rowiegar and Midhowe have walls extending from their ends and curving as though they were going to come together in a circle; at the latter site a gap in each wall may have been for access. At Unstan at least two walls had been butted against the tomb before the final skin of masonry was built around it. In the light of Isbister it seems much more reasonable that these walls delineated forecourts than that they were, for example, boundary walls connected with land use. More conventional hornworks can be seen in the form of the cairns of Fara, Knowe of Lairo, Head of Work, Point of Cott

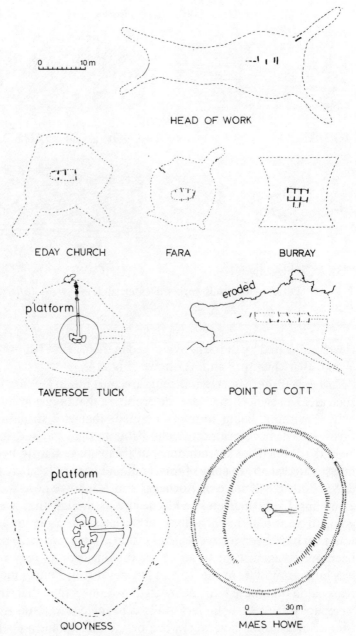

0 _____ 10 m

HEAD OF WORK

EDAY CHURCH   FARA   BURRAY

platform

TAVERSOE TUICK   POINT OF COTT

eroded

platform

QUOYNESS   MAES HOWE

0 _____ 30 m

Fig. 15   Forecourts and platforms (*after A.S. Henshall*)

and Eday Church (Fig. 15) though it is not known whether these were originally long enough to encompass an area. An interesting variation is where the tomb is known to be within the bounds of such an area. Colin Renfrew has demonstrated convincingly that Maes Howe was encircled by a bank 100 m in diameter within which a shallow ditch had been excavated. Similarly, at Taversoe Tuick and Quoyness the tombs were found to be surrounded by irregular platforms of stone and at the latter site this had been built before the final skin of the cairn had been put in place. All the examples cited with hornworks have stalled chambers while those with platforms or surrounded by a bank have Maes Howe and Bookan type interiors.

At Isbister there can be no doubt that all or part of the roof of the main chamber was removed prior to it being intentionally filled. This discovery entirely vindicates Henshall's argued case for the deliberate infilling of several of the Orkney tombs, bringing the total number of instances known to at least ten. Petrie had been aware of the possibility as early as 1849 for in describing his work at Wideford Hill he said:

> The appearance of the central chamber and its contents when examined was extremely puzzling for the animal remains lay intermingled with stones and earth, which presented unmistakeable evidence of having been poured down through a square opening in the apex of the building until the chamber was about two-thirds filled. It has been supposed that this was the debris of a superstructure which had crowned the Picts-house, and that it had found its way to the cell beneath; but the round shape of the top of the structure, its perfect appearance, the total absence of any trace of a superstructure, and, above all, the limited dimensions of the aperture through which the earth and stones alone could have entered the chamber, are all against the supposition and render it more than probable that whatever may have been the object contemplated by the act the contents of the chamber were purposely deposited therein by human hands.

Equally, however, it is certain that some of the chambers were not filled in for the Norsemen were able to write on the walls of Maes Howe, and Barry could view the bones on the chamber floor at Quanterness without having to excavate down to them.

The outer end of the entrance passage at Isbister had been destroyed by quarrying but it could be seen from its fill of wind-blown sandy soil that it had never been blocked. At other sites, however, there is evidence that entrances were blocked with masonry and other debris and in at least two cases this contained human bones. Such blocking may well have been intended to have been as permanent as the method of filling the chamber was but the entrances of the Dwarfie Stane, the Calf of Eday NW, and Maes Howe were all furnished with stones of appropriate size which could conceivably have been taken out and put back at will.

Finally there is some evidence for compartments within chambers having been sealed off either temporarily or permanently. The damaged side cell at Isbister was sealed from inside the chamber, though it is uncertain when this was done. At the Calf of Eday NW entry to the end compartment was blocked by masonry almost to the roof while each of the side cells at Maes Howe had its own blocking stone. Though the material remains of this phenomenon are not common the practice might have been quite usual and widespread; compartments may have gone in and out of use.

The era of the tombs: factors governing their siting

It is necessary first of all to clarify when the tombs were built and what their duration of use was. Typologies, including those of finds, are of little use here since they are interpretive and the main weapon in our armoury is radiocarbon dating. This notwithstanding, a small number of artefacts *are* of interest, ironically because they are not neolithic in date. We have also at this stage to decide what constitutes 'use'. The runic inscriptions inside Maes Howe would not come under this heading but it is known that at Isbister a great timespan elapsed between the intensive use of the chamber and its infilling and that even centuries thereafter the site was a focus of interest. 'Use' is therefore interpreted broadly here as meaning the period over which the tombs acted in some way as ritual centres, whether this involved their chambers or not.

Fortunately, radiocarbon dates from a number of sources exist. There are some from Isbister itself, a good series from Quanterness and Colin Renfrew has dated other samples from a number of earlier excavations and from the ditch at Maes Howe (Fig. 16). The earliest dates for Isbister suggest it was built around 3150 BC and there is a remarkable concurrence here with Quanterness where a sample of organic earth, which post-dated the building of the tomb but which pre-dated any burials, gave a single date of 3420 ($\pm$ 110) BC. These dates admittedly only relate to two tombs but advance dates from Pierowall Quarry on Westray also suggest that the main phase of building such monuments was in the last half of the fourth millennium BC. With further dates more precision may be attained, but it is to be noted that those obtained by Renfrew from bones found in the Knowe of Yarso, Knowe of Rowiegar, Knowe of Ramsay and Quoyness indicate that the tombs themselves must have been built by 3000 BC. It does seem reasonable, even on the basis of a sample of only six or seven sites, to suggest that the chambered tombs of Orkney were all built during a relatively short timespan and it is doubly interesting that at least the Maes Howe, stalled and hybrid types seem to be broadly coeval.

When it comes to the period of use Isbister and Quanterness are, again, our main sources of information. The chamber of the first was filled in around 2400 BC and the last date for bones from the second was 2430 ($\pm$ 90) BC. This gives spans of 800 ($\pm$ 80) and 990 ($\pm$200) years. There are obviously complications, not the least of which are that the bones from Isbister have dates which fall early in the period for which the chamber was open

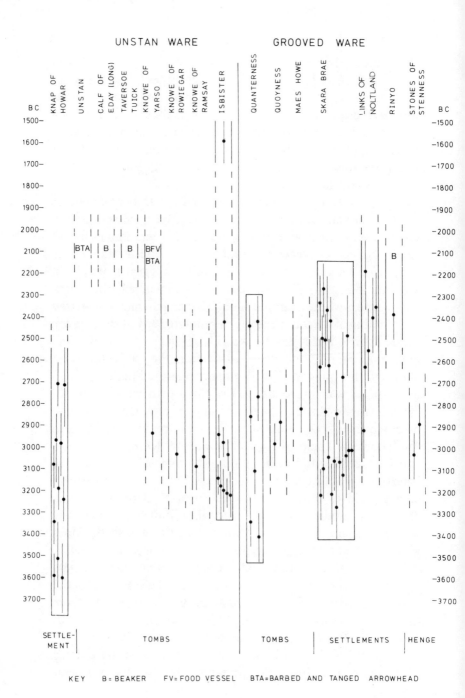

while those from Quanterness relate only to the last 550 ($\pm$ 180) years but the idea of their having generally been open for extended timespans is corroborated by Renfrew's determinations on samples from the older excavations, as can be seen from Fig. 16. It will also be seen from this that certain tombs had associated with them artefacts which have to be dated after 2100 BC, the beginning of the Bronze Age in Orkney. At Unstan a barbed and tanged arrowhead was in the chamber; at the Calf of Eday Long a piece of Beaker pottery; and at the Knowe of Yarso a further piece together with part of a Food Vessel and another barbed and tanged arrowhead. It is interesting that the chamber at the last site is one of those which Henshall considers to have been filled; the artefactual evidence, therefore, suggests that this was not done until the neolithic period was at an end. Interest in the site of tombs, if not the chambers themselves, would seem to have continued into the succeeding period. At Taversoe Tuick a Beaker-like vessel was found outside the upper entrance passage while what appear to have been Bronze Age burials were inserted into the top storey. At Isbister itself the remarkably late date of 1595 ($\pm$ 110) BC has been given for the disarticulated bones in the 'cist' behind the north hornwork. It does look as though the chambered tombs were of importance for a very long time indeed.

But why were the tombs put where they were in the first place? What were the factors which were of importance to the builders and which dictated what was a good or a bad site in their terms? For an answer to these questions it is necessary to turn to one of the most important facets of David Fraser's recent work on the Orkney tombs as a whole. His fieldwork was carried out with meticulous and comprehensive care and, having decided that seventy-six sites could be justifiably classified as chambered cairns, he set about exploring the relationship between each and the landscape on which they had been imposed. He made notes on the location and surroundings of

Fig. 16 Calibrated radiocarbon dates for the Orcadian Neolithic

every site and was able to evaluate this data by reference to information culled from various modern detailed studies. In doing so he assumed that the environment of Orkney, in its broadest sense, had not changed significantly between the neolithic period and the present day. Throughout his work he was looking for indications that the tomb builders had chosen locations and he was able to demonstrate this by showing that the chambered tombs in his sample were, in certain respects, far from randomly situated.

Table 1   The location of the chambered tombs relative to the surface geology of Orkney (*after D. Fraser*)

	% Area of Orkney	% Location of tombs
Sandstone	39.1	85.5
Peat	17.9	2.6
Boulder Clay	37.1	9.2
Miscellaneous	5.9	2.6

In the first part of his analysis he looked at the relationship between the tombs and single aspects of their environs. One key factor in determining location seems to have been the availability of building stone. As can be seen from Table 1 sixty-five of the cairns were located directly on sandstone, far more than if their distribution had been random, and Fraser further noted that some of those on boulder clay were close to sources of building stone and that none of the remainder was further than 1 km from bare rock. It may be remarked that here, as elsewhere, the low number of tombs found in peaty regions is attributed to some having been obscured since neolithic times. Another factor of interest is the relationship between the tomb and soils of differing type and potential (Table 2). Fraser found that they had been placed preferentially on what are now podzolic types and that the tendency was for them not to be built on gleys. It is not necessary to go into the intricacies of soil science in order to point out the importance of this finding. Gleys are fertile but wet and, without drainage, they would have

Table 2   The location of the chambered tombs relative to the soils of Orkney (*after D. Fraser*)

	% Area of Orkney	% Location of tombs
Podzols & P Complexes	38.9	72.4
Gleys & G Complexes	39.9	25.0
Peat	14.4	2.6
Miscellaneous	6.6	0

been too heavy to be tilled by neolithic man. Conversely what are now podzols, and relatively infertile, would, in neolithic times, have had a much better, and lighter, structure and it looks as though the tombs were located near what were then farmlands. The distribution of the chambered cairns is so dispersed that it seems reasonable to follow Fraser in his suggestion that each cairn may have been associated with a particular patch of farming land.

David Fraser then wondered whether the cairns might not have been specially positioned with regard to the shape, or topography, of the land around them. He found that, in fact, their location was very variable with examples on coastal plains, hill slopes, small islands or peninsulas, valley bottoms, the edges of natural terraces and, in lesser numbers, on hill and ridge tops and at the end of promontories. Further, while there was no seeming significance in their absolute altitudes, it did look as though they had been placed in either high or low positions with regard to the land immediately around. He then went on to examine the visibility from each tomb – this also giving an indication of the visibility *of* each tomb. He discovered that they had not been located in positions where visibility was restricted but that the emphasis was most commonly on being able to see – and be seen within – a distance of no more than 5 km. Like most man-built things in Orkney the tombs tended to be near the sea, or one of the large inland lochs, but a definite preference was shown in choosing between different types of coastline, high cliffs being favoured and beaches practically ignored. Moreover, the chosen sites were all easily accessible.

As far as can be seen, then, from the analysis so far the typical tomb was near a source of stone, associated with farmland, and in a position that was both singular but easily accessible and readily visible, even if only from a fairly local area. As it happens Isbister fits this picture exactly but the variability that exists elsewhere indicates that such a perfect siting was not always available for those who built tombs.

David Fraser was concerned lest the isolation and discussion of single aspects of tomb location be artificial. In making any decision all the factors involved are taken into account rather than considered individually and are weighed one against the other. His aim was to probe the complexities of thought of the neolithic builders. Accordingly he fed all the information he had obtained into a computer which had been programed to sort through the 1,672 entries and not only to group information in the form of significant factors but also to evaluate their relative importance. There were seven factors of which the five least important will be taken first and in descending order. The most significant of these, Factor III, was that the tomb should be away from peat but this is probably fallacious, for the reason already given. Factor IV was that the location should be in a high position with a distant panorama, though obviously only when this was possible. Factor V seemed to indicate a preference for cairns to be close to the rich pasture of established dune areas – thus corroborating the idea of their being near farmland. Factor VI was that they should be away from gleyic complexes, that is land that could not be used agriculturally. And Factor VII, the least important, was that there should be no extensive sectors of restricted visibility.

Factors I and II concerned the things that were uppermost in the minds of those choosing a site for their chambered cairn, and it is particularly interesting that Fraser was able to demonstrate that the first factor was of greater importance for those who built tombs which had simple – mostly stalled – chambers and which never had a very large cairn surrounding them. The implication is that the converse applies, i.e. that the second factor was of greater significance in the case of tombs with more complex chambers and larger – eventual – cairns. The two most important factors deciding sitings were as follows:

> *Factor I*: some distance from the shore, near the top of a hill but with the slope blocking an all-round panorama, with building stone easily accessible, and on or very close to land not now considered suitable for agriculture.
>
> *Factor II*: on good farming land of the present day with podzolic soils developed on glacial till and extensive views of land within 5 km.

In both cases the importance of a view over, and a view from, what would have been, at least potentially, farmland can be seen. The difference is that the tombs with smaller chambers and cairns were on the least viable of that land. They were more peripheral, or marginal, in terms of the economy of the times.

Tribal Orkney I

The time has now come to think about the distribution of the tombs in its broadest sense. As the accompanying map (Fig. 17) shows, they are not in one or more particular areas of Orkney but are scattered throughout the isles. Higher densities might be expected on fertile land but the concentrations that do exist on the distribution map have more to do with the interest that there has been in these areas than with anything else. This is especially clear in the case of Grant's work on Rousay and that of Petrie, Hebden, Farrer and Calder on Eday and the Calf. Yet the idea that the tombs were spread fairly evenly throughout Orkney has been given great support by the results of recent, intensive, impartial, and comprehensive surveying. One might be forgiven for thinking that chambered tombs would be

Fig. 17   Distribution of known chambered tombs in Orkney; land over 60 m stippled (after *D. Fraser*)

impossible to overlook but it is a fact that between Henshall's original published list of 1963 – itself a great advance – and Fraser's catalogue of 1983 the number of sites identified as neolithic tombs increased by almost 50 per cent, from 55 to 76. Moreover, many of these 'new' sites were in blank areas of the map. Stronsay now has five tombs where it formerly had one, Shapinsay has three rather than one, and South Ronaldsay has four where formerly Isbister alone was known – and that was not discovered until 1958.

It is this phenomenon of spacing that provides the initial insight into the type of society that lay behind the tombs when they were first erected. Childe's perceptive comment that there were almost as many chambered cairns on Rousay as there were farms in his day has already been mentioned. It has been seen from Fraser's analysis that they were universally close to or on pockets of farmland. Social anthropology must now act as our guide to further understanding. First, however, it will be helpful to make a short digression on the subject of tribes in general.

As the American social anthropologist Marshall D. Sahlins has said: 'The Neolithic was the historic day of tribesmen.' This pre-emptive statement allows us to view the condition of tribalism in a broad historic perspective as one stage in an evolutionary scale of social organisation. Prior to the neolithic period, man in Europe subsisted by hunting, fishing and gathering and it has been suggested that as much as 10 sq km of land would have been needed to support every individual. While these Mesolithic people would have been in groups or bands, other contact would have been infrequent and their social organisation simple. The 'Neolithic Revolution', however, involved the domestication of both plants and animals and, with farming, the selfsame land would have been capable of supporting about fifty times more people. This larger population would obviously have necessitated the more intricate ordering of social relations; interaction was greater, there was need of control over resources, and the greater number of goods generally associated with a sedentary life needed to be protected. Before going on to discuss this level of social organisation it must be said that it, too, was replaced. One then got civilisation as such and the nub of the difference between this and primitive societies is the formation of the state – the transfer of authority in general to a government which is above the bulk of the population and in which the control of law and order is largely invested. This permitted the evolution of larger social units within which 'civilisation', as we define it, could flourish.

It is Europe's prehistory that has been under consideration but tribal societies, and those of hunter-gatherers, have been observed in other parts of the world and many still exist. The general thinking here is that while certain levels of social organisation may have been supplanted in what may be called core areas some societies on the global peripheries have remained unaffected. The idea which follows this is that analysis of these societies will go a long way to elucidate our own prehistory if the information derived from social anthropology on the one hand and from archaeology on the other is handled with sufficient insight and sensitivity.

It has been observed that tribal society is liable to certain stresses but that centralisation of power came only with civilisation. Before this the resolution of stress lay with the individual and Sahlins, himself following Hobbes, has typified tribal societies as being in a constant condition of *Warre*. This must not be taken to mean that they are constantly fighting – indeed tribes may be peaceful, just as civilisations can be warlike. What the word expresses is a potential which is endemic in the system and what is of interest is the social mechanisms that exist in order to control it. An appreciation of this situation helps explain what may seem at first sight to be rather weird behaviour on the part of tribesmen, both recent and long past.

In what is commonly called economics, for example, tribesmen have little concept of the market or of making a profit in financial terms. To take advantage would be to provoke trouble and this is given a wide berth, needed items being gained through processes in which the social element can almost entirely efface the commercial. This goes to the extreme of people exchanging sometimes identical objects with little regard to whether either party wants or needs what it gets. The process is primarily one of establishing or of perpetuating good social relations. Equally, the idea of someone simply giving away part or all of their disposable wealth might seem surprising to our own culture but to an affluent tribesman this is very sensible indeed; the recipients are not only his friends, they are also indebted to him and what was disposable and often perishable has not only raised him in the eyes of other men but has been converted to a deposit of social obligation which he may call upon at will.

Kinship, too, is a vital mechanism – perhaps the most vital – and it pervades the structure of tribal societies; to the tribesman there are kin – with whom he has defined relationships – and strangers – with whom he doesn't. What effectively happens is that the idea of kinship is taken far beyond the bounds immediately recognisable to our society so as to take in as many people as possible. Your parents' siblings may also notionally be your mother and father, their children be regarded as your own brothers and sisters, and so on. Tribal divisions tend to follow lineages which profess common descent and which are often located in their own areas. One might think that oppositions could grow between such groups but marriage is regulated so as to join them in a web of kinship. The upshot of all this is that interaction is governed by family ties rather than anything more volatile. If a dispute should occur so many people become involved – all having ties with each other – that there is a tendency for the whole matter to be smoothed over rather than settled by conflict.

Thirdly, there are public, communal rituals – a usual feature of tribal life. Whatever a ceremony is about it reinforces the social structure, providing a focus of attention for the group involved and giving it identity and unity. Ceremonies are often concerned with things which are of immediate importance to tribesmen such as their gods, totems, territories, and ancestors – in so far as these can be distinguished. Ceremonies may also sublimate rivalry between groups, substituting the magnificence of ritual and the competitive squandering of resources, whether of labour or of produce.

But tribes do differ and while it is possible to generalise, to work out an average type, it is more appropriate here to look at the two extremes of our posited line of social evolution. In doing so the published work of Marshall D. Sahlins serves as a guide. Starting at the lower end, first segmentary tribes, constituting a bare advance over hunters, will be examined. At the other extreme, just short of states, there are chiefdoms; these will be discussed in due course. It must be remembered that in reality there are a large number of types between these polar opposites.

A segmentary tribe is fragmented socially and politically. Its component parts are small, independent, local communities which may inhabit a village, scattered hamlets, or a dispersed arrangement of homesteads. Whichever the case, they lie within the territory of the community and in almost all instances this is diminutive in size. The number of people involved may be a hundred or more but it is frequently less. They may belong to a single descent group, such as a lineage, or may be an association of several such groups; sometimes they are little more than a loose kindred. Whatever the structure, the pattern is repeated throughout the tribe and each unit is by and large autonomous. They eat and use what they produce and make with relatively little exchange. For this reason territories usually take in a share of all the main resources, be they sea, arable land, pasture or rock. They are also politically equal, thinking of themselves as independent and recognising no superior power. Leadership within them is restricted. There are sometimes petty chieftains who, by virtue of descent or age, are spokesmen and masters of ceremonies but who have no privileges and little influence. Alternatively, or in addition, there may be 'big men' who temporarily lead by virtue of their charisma, prowess, or the wealth of social obligations they have amassed but whose rule is transitory. Alliances between groups may come about in pursuit of particular objectives but when the reason has passed each becomes autonomous once more. In general the only links are those of kinship though this may be formalised into such pan-tribal institutions as clans, non local groups claiming common descent through one means or another. Generally speaking, however, this is a type of society which is extremely decentralised. The local groups are all important, being very jealous of their territory, identity, and sovereignty; higher levels of organisation scarcely exist.

Colin Renfrew contends that the former existence of such societies can be recognised in the archaeological record. The conditions are threefold. First, one has to be able to establish a pattern of contemporary sites whose location indicates spacing rather than clustering – and in this sense mutual repulsion rather than attraction. The areas around such sites can be considered as territories. Second, one has to be sure that the sites relate to the activities of the people in whose territory they lay – rather than being the product of cross-cutting groups. And third, there must be no hierarchy of sites which can be interpreted as indicating a social and political hierarchy.

The tombs of Orkney provide an almost ideal example of such a phenomenon. There is reason to believe that their initial building happened at more or less the same time and it is known that they do not cluster. As will be seen, there is evidence that in the early stage of their use, at least, they housed the remains of the dead of whole communities rather than those of particular sections. The third factor is difficult to evaluate, for reasons which will be apparent, but it can be hypothesised that when first built the tombs had an equivalence.

Now, it is in the nature of archaeology that more is known about the tombs in some areas than in others. Rather than thinking of Orkney as a whole, therefore, it seems expedient to follow Renfrew's example in considering the island about which most is known – Rousay. The distribution of the tombs here at first makes little sense but if the contours of the island and the arable land are added to its coastal outline then the sites of interest can be seen to be scattered either on or on the margins of the low-lying peripheral farmland (Fig. 18). If lines bisecting the distance between neighbouring tombs are then drawn notional territories (Thiessen polygons) are arrived at and it will be observed that these all cut across the grain of the landscape.

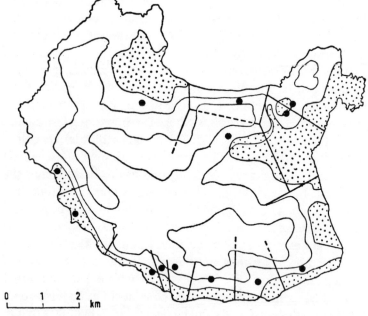

0   1   2
└───────┴───────┘ km

Fig. 18 Rousay with known tombs shown in relation to modern
arable land, contours, and coastline and with hypothetical territories
marked in (*after C. Renfrew*)

Some of the territories so defined are smaller than others, in
consequence of tombs being close together, and the possibility
that the sites in question either succeeded one another or that
they all belonged to the same residential group must be borne in
mind. Although it is not intended to pursue this line of thought
further here, it takes little imagination to envisage similar
territories for the tombs of other parts of Orkney. One can, for
instance, stand at Isbister and look across the land, thinking in a
very positive way about where the territory of that particular
tomb may have ended and what resources would have lain
within the area involved.

In such an area there would have been the homes of the
community which centred itself on the tomb. Only a little is
known about neolithic dwellings in Orkney – not nearly as

much as about the tombs – since houses would be more easily destroyed and less easily found. There are, however, other ways of estimating the size of the communities involved. For instance, the extent of a community's territory gives an indication of the size of population that might have been supported. Renfrew pursued this using modern ethnographic parallels from Africa. Taking into account the area of arable land and potential for grazing, and giving allowance for the former to be rested, he came to the conclusion that each of the Rousay territories may have been the province of between twenty-five and fifty people and that the population of the island as a whole would have been between 300 and 650. On their own such figures could be considered only to provide an order of magnitude but they are, in fact, corroborated by information from a second source. At Quanterness it was estimated that some 394 people had been buried in the tomb altogether; bone analysis showed the average age of death to have been about twenty years; and radiocarbon dating indicated that the tomb had been in active use for around 550 ($\pm$ 180) years. It is possible to work out from these figures that the tomb of Quanterness may have contained all the dead of a group with an average membership of between thirteen and twenty individuals. Similarly, it is known that at Isbister a total of some 341 burials were involved; the average age of death was nineteen years and eleven months; and the chamber was used intensively for 160 ($\pm$ 160) years. This in turn implies an average population of at least twenty-one people over sixteen generations but with a greater likelihood of it having been forty-two people over eight. The third insight comes from the few settlements that are known. Skara Brae, as it is now seen, is a hodgepodge of different phases of occupation but even if five of the houses were in use at one time it seems unlikely that they accommodated a total of more than fifty people. Rinyo, though not fully excavated, can be thought of on the same scale but Knap of Howar is smaller, consisting of only two structures. Taking everything into consideration the figure of twenty-five to fifty people does seem to be a reasonable estimate of the size of the communities that inhabited the territories within which each tomb lay. If all the tombs have been located – which is unlikely – then the population of Orkney as a whole at the time must have been between 1,600 and 3,200. If half the tombs are known, which seems probable from their distribution, then the figures can be doubled. It was, then, a small-scale society at both community and tribal level. And, lest it should be thought that such figures are all in the imagination, it might be remembered that the rural population of Orkney *now* is only 12,000, just twice the estimated maximum for the neolithic period.

The question must be raised whether such small groups had within them the manpower necessary to build a chambered tomb. Although the answer that will be reached here is that they did, this should be taken merely as illustrating the possibility, for the whole concept will later be qualified. The figure required is the number of man-hours involved and Renfrew gave a very good lead by obtaining data on traditional Orcadian quarrying and drystone building practice from a retired country builder. From this source we have the following figures (which are here converted to metric):

1 A quarryman could take out 7.8 cu m of rock in an eight-hour day.
2 1 cu m of living rock, however, becomes 4.5 cu m of compact rubble. This would have had to be shifted from the quarry to the building site and here the builder was able only to give figures for when barrows were used. In an eight-hour day a man could be expected to *either* load 9.88 cu m *or* take barrows containing some 14.44 cu m a distance of around 23 m. Any levelling required could be done at the rate of 28.88 cu m a working day.
3 A due allowance would have to be made for setting out the building but a mason was expected to build 3.04 cu m in an eight-hour day. For each such cu m of masonry 3.67 cu m of rubble would have been used.

As it happens, more is known about the construction of Isbister than of any other site and the above figures can be used to work out how long it would have taken to build *if this had taken place earlier this century*. In Table 3 figures are rounded off (thus introducing certain discrepancies) and a notional amount has been added in to cover the labour involved in preparing the site by digging out the natural bank at the south end of where the chamber was to be.

A mid-twentieth-century builder would then have put in an estimate of around 6,000 man-hours to build just such a tomb as that at Isbister. His men would, however, have had the benefit of metal tools and wheelbarrows and in projecting the figures back to the neolithic period I feel they should be at least doubled: 12,650 hours represents an enormous amount of effort. To have such a tomb built nowadays in neolithic fashion and on land one owned would cost in the region of £35,000 – the price of building a reasonable-sized modern house, a very small church, or a prefabricated community centre. This last comment is made *not* because there is any direct equivalence but simply to reinforce appreciation of the scale of the undertaking.

The question still remains, could little groups of twenty-five to fifty individuals erect a construction of such a scale? Here two points brought out by Table 3 are worth mentioning. One is that the phases of building involved the same order of effort and that it is only necessary to take one of these into account at one time – the final tomb being a cumulative product. The second point is that while 10 per cent of the time involved was taken up with quarrying and 30 per cent with building and spreading, loading and shifting the materials took no less than 60 per cent. This means that more than half the construction work could have been carried out by the unskilled – by children, for example. For reasons which will be gone into later, it would seem that only some 40 per cent of the population at Isbister would have been over the age of fifteen, the remainder being children. In a group of twenty-five to fifty one would thus expect an average of ten to twenty adults, both men and women. These adults would

Table 3 Number of man-hours that Isbister would have required to be built in the earlier part of this century

| | Masonry etc (cu m) | MAN-HOURS | | | | | |
		Quarrying	Loading	Shifting	Spreading	Building	Totals
1st phase							
Site preparation	5	5	18	12	6	—	42
First skin	210	176	624	427	—	553	1779
Total	215	181	624	439	6	553	1821
2nd phase							
Second skin	340	284	1010	691	—	895	2881
3rd phase							
Masonry hornworks	125	105	371	254	—	329	1059
Rubble backing	300	68	243	166	83	—	560
Total	425	173	614	420	83	329	1619
Totals		**638**	**2266**	**1550**	**89**	**1777**	**6321**

have had to do at least 50 per cent of the work involved in constructing the tomb and if the second – the largest – phase of building is taken this means that they would have had to put in 115 to 230 hours each. Just three to six weeks. Clearly it *was* possible for such a group to have built a tomb unaided but, even disregarding later qualifications, it would seem probable that kinsmen from other groups would have been drafted in with inducements of feasts or in order to pay off previous social obligations.

Is it possible to go further? Is it permissible to generalise from this information about Isbister in order to throw light on the labour investment involved in the other tombs known of in Orkney? The answer is that it is – *but* at the general level to be taken it is possible only to talk of tombs as built finally, rather than their phases of construction, and any calculations will incorporate large degrees of error. The effect on total manhours that distance from a quarry would have had has already been seen and there are other factors of equally great importance about which insufficient information is available in most instances. It would not be appropriate to burden a text such as this with too many figures but it is felt necessary to show the basis of the computations lest they be credited with more confidence than they deserve.

The best type of information available is from tombs which have been investigated sufficiently for both the shape of the chamber and that of the original cairn to be known. If it is assumed, on the evidence of Isbister, that the outer cairn face was near vertical then multiplying the basal area by the original height of the tomb will give its overall volume. If from this is deducted the volume of the chamber – roughly its area by its height – then the total number of cubic metres of masonry involved is calculated. Now, if the first and second phases at Isbister are taken, i.e. the tomb as such, then – using doubled labour figures – it can be seen that 550 cu m of masonry took 9,300 hours to erect and that 1 cu m would therefore have taken an average of just on seventeen hours. Multiplying this figure by the volume of masonry in any other tomb gives an estimate of the labour involved – though taking no account of differing conditions. This all seems very easy but the fact of the matter is that little information is available on the original height of either chambers or cairns. This problem, however, can be overcome – though only by introducing more errors. It seems likely that the original height of chambers was related to their width because of the way corbelling was used to take their walls up to a point where they could be capped with flagstones. The six chambers where the height can be surmised were therefore taken – Isbister, Quanterness, Holm of Papa Westray S, Quoyness, Knowe of Lairo and Maes Howe – and this figure was plotted against their width. The result was encouraging and a line was drawn through the graph so that an estimate for the height of any other chamber could be obtained providing its width was known. It must, however, be stressed that the figures obtained could be 0.5 m or more in error. An estimated height for the cairn was then calculated for each site by arbitrarily adding 50 cm to the figure for the chamber ceiling.

The second class of information is from tombs where the size and shape of the chamber is known but where the original cairn has remained masked by tumbled material derived from it. In the case of both Quanterness and Maes Howe it is known that the original area of these tombs was only, on average, 45 per cent of that of the mound which eventually formed and this figure was therefore used as a correction factor. In the third category of information the problem of a masked cairn is compounded by our not having information on the width and area of the chamber. The only possible solution to this was to use the forty tombs in the first two classes to provide an average height for cairns and an average volume for chambers. Fourthly, and finally, there are tombs of which little is known. There are only six of these but it has also to be taken into account that many more tombs will have existed than are at present known. It would be unwise to ignore this.

In addition to the above considerations a number of loose

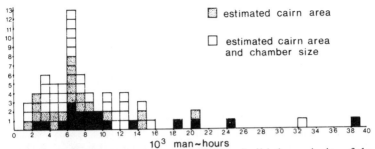

Fig. 19   Estimated man-hours required to build the majority of the chambered tombs known in Orkney

ends had to be allowed for while making the calculations. It was not possible, for example, to obtain a figure for the Dwarfie Stane on Hoy, and computations for the subterranean and double-decker tombs will have been far from perfect – though, in the event, neither matters much. The figures arrived at have been plotted in the form of a histogram (Fig. 19). The first thing apparent is the extremely wide range of labour commitment there seems to have been. All the sites in the sample may well be subsumed under the general title of 'chambered cairn' but, at the one extreme, the Calf of Eday NW took only around 1,200 man-hours to complete while, at the other, Maes Howe would have involved an estimated 38,800. The second point to be revealed is that the tombs of our sample are very unevenly distributed along this line of manpower involvement. The histogram is skewed towards low values with a great clump of tombs which apparently took less than 10,000 man-hours to build – forty-eight of the sixty-nine in the sample – and with larger ones being markedly less frequent with increased size. A third point that should be noted is that the shape of the histogram has remained unaltered with the addition of figures which contain a high level of estimation. This gives confidence in these figures but it also means that tombs of all sizes remain to be investigated fully – including one approaching the size of Maes Howe. As will be seen, the ability to choose a tomb of a particular scale for examination may be of great significance.

Tribal Orkney II

Colin Renfrew's example has been followed in positing that when the tombs were first built they were the product of equal and autonomous groups within a segmentary tribal society. It has further been conjectured, however, that there would have been competition between these groups, some faring better than others, and that this may have been expressed through the aggrandisement of the monument which was a symbol of their being. Now it will be seen that some of the tombs were indeed much grander than others. But, is this the total explanation of the phenomenon? Could it not be that some groups surpassed others in more than a symbolic sense? Might not the enlargement of some tombs be an indicator of the transformation of an egalitarian society to one which was hierarchically structured? The demonstration of such a process of stratification would be very exciting but, before it is attempted, reference should be made to a cultural division the existence of which we are already aware. The fact is that although the Maes Howe, tripartite and stalled, and hybrid forms of chamber were in use contemporaneously the Maes Howe type is associated with one form of pottery (Grooved Ware) and the stalled, tripartite and, seemingly, hybrid, with another (Unstan Ware). These classes of pottery also divide the settlement sites and these in turn incorporate differences in building style. We do not have such information for the tombs with Bookan type chambers though this is relatively unimportant, from the present perspective, because of their smallness of numbers and scale. What is important is an understanding that the neolithic population of Orkney can be divided into two major parts on the basis of some elements of their material cultures. It is probable that they originated from different areas and, after all that has been said about segmentary societies, there is no difficulty in imagining their ability to coexist. But, to revert to our former question, it might be wondered whether these sub-cultural groupings continued to be of significance in any social stratification or centralisation that came to pass.

At this stage it would be possible to examine the distribution of all the known tombs from the point of their subcultural affinity but this will be omitted for two reasons. In the first place this distribution provides a test whereby the conclusions that are to be reached can be evaluated. And, secondly, those conclusions do a great deal to help us understand what seems otherwise to be a very muddled picture. A start will be made, therefore, by considering not all the tombs, but just those which are thought to have taken more than 10,000 man-hours to build – this being a figure taken arbitrarily – identifying them, where possible, with the subcultural groupings known. If these are plotted on a map of Orkney – bearing in mind that some will be missing – it will be found that their distribution is noticeably dispersed. Evidently, it was not a case of tombs in a particular area of the islands being enlarged but of this happening to just one in each of a number of groups throughout the tribal territory as a whole. Such nucleation or stratification as can be seen at this stage was localised and an idea of the size of the amalgamated territories involved can be obtained by the previously discussed means of drawing Thiessen polygons. The borders of these should not be taken literally; they are merely a geometrically based aid to thought. In addition to helping us over individual territories it will be observed that they give an insight into the areas of the two subcultural groupings, though the presence of a number of tombs with uncertain affiliation is – for the moment – vexing.

Once having established the process it can be followed through by making plots of tombs at increasing levels of manpower input (Fig. 20). The figures taken are, again, entirely arbitrary, being 15,000+, 20,000+ and 25,000+ man-hours. At each stage the distribution remains as dispersed as can be and from this it can be concluded that there was a coalescing of territories at a local level of increasing scale. This theoretical conclusion, however, can be seen to be based very much in reality for not only do the smaller territories unite to make larger

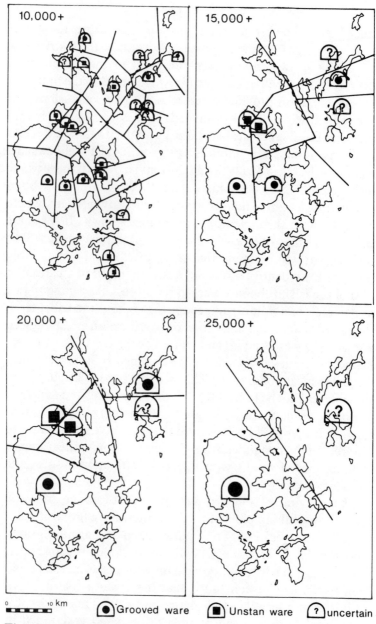

Fig. 20 Hypothetical man-hour territories of increasing scale associated with tombs in Orkney

ones with roughly the same boundaries but those of the different subcultures remain as discrete as is possible. For the moment we will leave Orkney at the point where it is divided into two parts: the Mainland and the South Isles dominated by Maes Howe, and the North Isles by the Earl's Knoll on Papa Stronsay (which is of uncertain type, but which will be supposed to have belonged to the Unstan Ware subculture). We will leave, too, the question of how the various tribal subdivisions were affected though with present knowledge of such societies it seems probable that coalescence occurred along real or fictitious kinship lines, higher and higher groupings being related to an increasingly removed supposed common ancestry. Now is the time to go back to the beginning and to see if the clustering observed and the original distribution of tomb types are compatible and if they throw light on each other.

This will be done by overlaying one on the other but to obtain the maximum returns from the exercise it would be well to follow a few common-sense rules. In the first place our territorial boundaries ought to be invariable; that is, the product of two or three territories combining should occupy exactly the same space as its component parts did. Second, mathematically derived territorial boundaries are not likely to reflect reality too closely and it seems justifiable to alter their course slightly, as necessary, in order to take account of natural factors such as straits, hills, and the discreteness of islands. This is kept to a minimum. Third, areas with mixed subcultural sites – including habitations – should be seen as being on boundaries, this being the least sensitive position they could be in. Finally, some licence may be permitted to add hypothetical territories where evidence is scant. As will be seen, this applies only to West Mainland and the Burray/South Ronaldsay group of islands.

The results obtained are shown in the accompanying map (Fig. 21) and, without undue exaggeration, can be said to be quite staggering. There is no significant conflict between the overall distribution of tombs by subcultural type and the

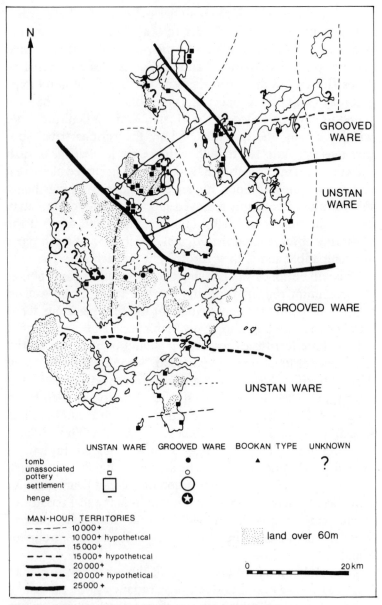

Fig. 21   Hypothetical tribal map of neolithic Orkney

territories obtained. Each of what might be called the 10,000+ man-hour territories can be seen to include lesser ones belonging to the same subculture and they too combined in a similar systematic way over the subcultural areas up to and including the 20,000+ man-hour stage. The subcultural areas are in turn well defined, with the Grooved Ware people having occupied Mainland and Sanday and North Ronaldsay, and with the Unstan Ware element of the population having been in the remaining North Isles and the cultivatable portions of the southern ones.

This original division of Orkney seems to have broken down to a certain extent by the time that the process of nucleation or stratification had reached the point where just two tombs exceeded the 25,000+ man-hour mark. Now, the actual man-hour figure obtained for Maes Howe is almost 39,000 while that for its counterpart, the Earl's Knoll, is just 32,000. If the line of argument used so far is followed the conclusion would be reached that at the highest level Orkney, and its subcultures, may have been united. Would this be pure fantasy? Or, is there anything to substantiate such a suggestion?

The ultimate in tomb size has been reached but within walking distance of Maes Howe there are the two henge sites of the Stones of Stenness and the Ring of Brodgar. The standing stone circles of these are their most immediately apparent feature but each was originally bounded by a deep rock-cut ditch, the material from this probably having been put to the outside to form a bank. Using figures from his builder-informant, Renfrew calculated that the ditch of the Ring of Brodgar would have taken about 75,000 man-hours to quarry in fairly recent times. If this figure is doubled, as it was in the case of the tombs, 150,000 man-hours is obtained as an estimate for the time it would have taken with the equipment available in the neolithic period. These figures, however, do not take any account of the labour that would have been required in making the conjectured outer bank and, more to the point, in quarrying, transporting, and erecting sixty large stones. The total would, in all probability, have been in excess of 200,000 hours. Stenness is much smaller, having a circumference of half that of Brodgar and containing only twelve stones, and therefore a figure of around 85,000 hours might be suggested for its construction. This estimate will be used, since it is based on similar information to all the others, but it is reassuring that it is corroborated to an acceptable degree by entirely independent work. Following Graham Ritchie's excavations at the Stones of Stenness, Ian Ralston used labour figures which had been worked out for similar monuments constructed in chalk areas. Using a factor of four to account for the different rock type he arrived at the figure of 50,000 hours – this being for quarrying the ditch and forming its outer bank, giving no allowance for work associated with the central stone circle.

Before discussing the importance of these figures the factors of subcultural affinity and date have to be taken into consideration. Colin Renfrew's work at the Ring of Brodgar yielded, unfortunately, no information on these points but Graham Ritchie showed the Stones of Stenness to be associated with Grooved Ware and he also obtained radiocarbon dates which indicated that it was constructed prior to 3038 (± 150) BC and that it continued in use through to at least 2134 (± 379) BC. The total information available about these two sites supports our thesis of centralisation in the Orcadian Neolithic in three ways. In the first place they are in the location which has been suggested became the focal point of the tribe as a whole; in the second, the subcultural identity is what would have been predicted; and, thirdly, under discussion are monuments which *clearly* could not have been built by the small, autonomous groups of people with which we started. It is possible to go further than that, for if the building of the henges does indicate centralisation then this must have been completed by 3000 BC. This means it happened over a comparatively short space of time, only 500 years, and, additionally, it clarifies our interpretation of a very important point.

The information presented relating larger and larger territories to the increasing man-hour input into fewer and fewer tombs could be taken to imply that chambered tombs were progressively abandoned and that uniting groups totally lost their independent identity. This seems unlikely, both because they were residential groups, and would still have had to relate to areas of farmland, and because the idea does not conform to what is known of tribes. Though there is no evidence for building after 3000 BC – except, conveniently, for the bank around Maes Howe, which was put up about this time – it is known that the tombs in general continued in use through the Late Neolithic, some even being of demonstrable significance into the Early Bronze Age. Here is not the annihilation of the identity of the small original groups but their welding into a hierarchically structured society. Despite its limitations, the map on p. 118 (Fig. 21) can therefore be looked upon as giving an idea of the hierarchy of tribal divisions that existed in Orkney from around 3000 BC to at least 2000 BC, when alterations may have occurred with the Bronze Age.

At this juncture social anthropology must again be turned to for help in appreciating what the structure of society would have been like. The one extreme of Sahlins' line of social evolution in tribes, segmentary societies, has been covered and the other, chiefdoms, must now be examined. In these the local groups are no longer egalitarian or autonomous but are hierarchically arranged and are each just part of a system which may, or may not, incorporate the whole of the tribe concerned. A chiefdom is essentially a ranked society and, because of the way tribes operate, the hierarchy most frequently finds expression in degrees of kinship. Thus, in a conical clan system the chiefs of existing local lineages are seen as the product of a largely mythical ancestry which ultimately links them to a common founder but which also gives them an order or precedence according to a rule of primogeniture. Hence, the eldest son of the eldest son of the eldest son of the ultimate ancestor will be chief of the whole area. But, at the next level down of chieftainship there will be the senior descendants of the sons of the ultimate ancestor, in order, including the one we already have, and these will have a lesser authority over subdivisions of the territory of the clan as a whole. The process extends through the senior descendants of the grandsons, great grandsons etc of the ultimate ancestor with smaller and smaller territories being involved until the level of the local lineage chiefs in total is reached. The local lineage chiefs in any one area will be subordinate to the most senior of them but he in turn is just one of several intermediate chiefs among whom there will be one superior by virtue of descent. Thus territories can be seen to coalesce with each stage of authority until the point is reached where they are unified under the direct descendant of the clan ancestor.

Although the process has been followed down to the lineage chiefs it must be said that status by descent does not stop there but permeates the whole of society. Even the last born of the last born of the lowest lineage has a nobility relative to his own children. Thus while a chiefdom may be a *ranked* society it is not a *class* one; there is no definite division between nobles and commoners and there is no complete arrogation of power and the means of production by a separate élite. It is all a matter of degree or, to use Sahlins' words, it is a system of 'graded familial priorities in the control of wealth and force, in claims to others' services, in access to divine power, and in material styles of life'.

It can be seen that it is very much a simplification to say that a chiefdom has a chief when in reality it is a system of chieftain-ship which involves a hierarchy of major and minor authorities over corresponding subdivisions of the tribe. The effect, for all that, is ultimate centralisation of authority and the chain of command gives a kinship-based political organisation which surpasses the community level to varying degrees and which links with, and enlarges, both economic and ceremonial life. Everyday production is still based on homesteads and villages but the chiefs at each territorial level may call upon goods and services and, in order to make this effective, pressure is applied – sometimes aided by diversification and specialisation – so that a surplus is produced. This levy is sometimes redirected downwards, in case of need – this supporting the position of the relevant chief – but is otherwise turned to keeping the nobility at each level and to providing the wherewithal for the carrying out of public works, the erection of monuments, and the staging of ceremonies of increasing magnificence. The paramount chief, for example, may levy goods from the whole tribe in order to support a court of nobles, priests, advisers, or whatever; he is in a position to authorise ceremonies which bind the group as a whole; and he can call upon massive amounts of labour if he thinks that a central temple, or such, needs to be built.

When the point came where the structure and working of a chiefdom had to be illustrated it occurred to me that the most informative way of doing this would be to combine what is known of the most typical type – the conical clan – with the information already derived for Orkney in the later Neolithic. After all, not only has a hierarchy of monument sizes, each dependent upon the volume of services that could be called upon, been established, but there is also a related one of coalescing territories. Though the archaeological conditions for supposing a chiefdom exist, it must be very firmly stated that, at this stage, there is no indication of whether it was constituted along the lines of a conical clan. The example given does, however, provide an idea of how such a society may have operated and this is very important because of the remoteness of this form of social structure from our everyday knowledge and way of thinking.

The lowest common denominator in neolithic Orkney is the individual tomb, associated with and within the territory of a farming community which was probably structured along kinship lines. In a conical clan any such community would have had its own chief, though this would be at quite a low level of organisation in the society as a whole. There were, then, at least seventy-six 'chiefs' in Orkney at any one time – though there would have been as many more as there are tombs which remain undiscovered. The next step up in our combined model would be that within a local area these petty chiefs would be related by lineage and that one would be superior by reason of descent. At this level he would have authority over the combined territories and would be able to call upon services from the wider area with the result that the tomb sited near the community he belonged to would be relatively large – 10,000+ man-hours. Though there are gaps in our knowledge it might be imagined that there were something like twenty-seven chiefs of this order at any one time, each having, say, two to five subordinate chiefs. These second-order chiefs would, however, have been in turn subordinate to the one among them in their area who had the closest link with the ultimate ancestor and, following our former reasoning, it will have been the communities of the chiefs of this third order that had near them the 15,000+ man-hour tombs. In the model there are eight, each having dominance over the combined territories of up to four local subordinates. The territories are very well defined in geographical terms at this stage but at the next, the fourth, as many as three are combined under the four most superior chiefs, these having control, respectively, over Mainland, North Ronaldsay and Sanday, the other North Isles, and the South Isles; next to the communities they belonged to were tombs which involved a labour input greater than others in the enlarged area. Here there were two chiefs for the Grooved Ware subculture and two for the Unstan Ware one; out of each pair one was superior by virtue of descent and his command over the whole subcultural area was indicated by, and resulted in, tombs involving more than 30,000 man-hours. Finally, some sort of lineage link appears to have been forged, in more senses than one, between the two subcultures with the Grooved Ware chief in the Maes Howe area being given absolute precedence.

All this has been derived from matching a conical tribal formation with a hierarchy of territories based on man-hour figures for monuments. The tribesmen involved would, however, have seen everything in terms of lineage and ancestry and I think that little harm is done by sketching this into our diagram

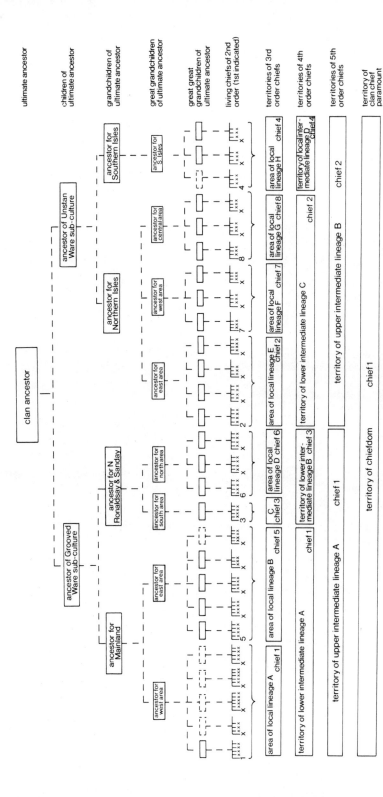

Fig. 22 The structure of a chiefdom such as may have existed in neolithic Orkney

in order to clarify it. Figure 22 creates a hypothetical model of society in Orkney in the late neolithic period, showing the mythical ancestry of the tribe, the order of precedence of the top twenty-seven chiefs, and the way in which territories were combined under those with closer and closer links to the clan founder.

4 · Rites for the Living

Ritual centres

In the last chapter I looked at the tombs and henges largely from the point of view of what they tell us about the structure of the society of their times. This, however, is only part of the picture that is required and I will now consider various aspects of the culture that existed – though it will be appreciated that these two facets of the social organisation as a whole are necessarily intertwined. One point that should be made at the outset is that there is no discernible difference in the culture – in the social anthropological sense – of the Grooved Ware and Unstan Ware people. It has been seen that the division was of significance in the social structure but it is only apparent from limited aspects of material culture and the evidence which follows shows it to have been subordinate to a tribal level of unity which took in the whole of Orkney.

The first indicator of this pan-Orcadian cultural unity is the universal existence of chambered tombs – whatever the details of their varied construction. The limited approach of sub-divisions and typology can be abandoned and the subject re-approached with the simple and ultimately more thought-provoking question of why the people built such structures. Moreover, it might be asked what was the function of the monuments erected in the society of the day? Superficially it might be imagined that they were for the dead but this is only a small part of the answer; in reality they were very much for the living.

Human beings, like a large number of other animal species, are very aware of the territory in which they live and they tend to identify with it and to resent encroachment upon its area and resources by people they regard as strangers having no title. This applies whether one is talking about individuals, their family, and their residential group or whether one is looking at the level of a tribe, or even that of a present-day nation. Tribesmen are particularly sensitive about their territorial identity, often adopting differences of custom, dress and mannerism as a constant reminder both to themselves and to their neighbours. Further, a grove, clearing, natural feature or more formalised ceremonial ground may be seen by the group involved as symbolising their territory as a whole, providing a focus for many of their more significant communal activities. There is here the beginnings of an explanation for the existence of the Orkney tombs: they were territorial markers.

It was Colin Renfrew who first argued this and he also gave considerable thought to the question of why such large monuments should have been erected at comparatively local levels. He noted that chambered tombs in general have a restricted distribution, being found only on the seaboard of the Atlantic and North Sea, and he wondered whether their occurrence there might not result from a condition common to the whole of this area in the neolithic period. The solution he found most satisfactory was concerned with population stress. The Neolithic Revolution meant that land could support more people and this would have triggered off a population explosion. There was always a potential danger here since a practical limit would inevitably be reached but this was not apparent until the coast – the 'Atlantic Façade' – stopped the process of emigration which would have relieved the situation elsewhere. Primitive populations are quite capable of limiting their rate of increase, as will be seen, but after generations had accommodated themselves to a different situation the necessity would have come as shock. It is this stress which Renfrew saw as having been behind an increased territorial sensitivity which provided just such an atmosphere as might be expected to spark off the building of monuments of great magnificence within the framework of a segmented tribal society. Indeed, it may be said that some of the closest existing parallels are the monuments of Polynesia – Easter Island in particular – and one can envisage these too as having been brought about through the medium of population crises. It is particularly instructive to appreciate that the rise of chiefdoms only exacerbates the situation in that land is made even more productive under administrative and political control. The problems of the early Neolithic would not therefore have been solved once and for all but would have recurred with the result that yet bigger monuments were built which related to the larger territories of the new social structure.

The chambered cairns of Orkney, as elsewhere, are usually referred to as tombs for the very good reason that their most common inclusion is human remains. It might be concluded from this that their primary function was simply the disposal of the dead but even at this level of analysis – here regarded as a relatively superficial one – there are problems. The two most recently excavated Orcadian chambered tombs, Isbister and Quanterness, were found to contain the bones of some 341 individuals and an estimated 394, respectively, and these numbers could certainly have been taken to support the thesis *if* they could be viewed in isolation and *if* the implications of the rather precise dating that exists were ignored. As it is, it is known that other excavated chambers contained remains of relatively few bodies – in Midhowe there were twenty-five, in the Knowe of Yarso twenty-nine, in the Knowe of Ramsay three, in Blackhammer two, and in the Calf of Eday Long one. These were all investigations of comparatively recent date and there is no reason to disbelieve their findings; at the same time they give credibility to the very patchy reporting of human remains from earlier excavations. The second problem is that the series of radiocarbon dates from Isbister and Quanterness indicate a discrepancy between the length of time during which the chambers were open and the period during which the bones which have been recovered were deposited. In the case of Isbister it would seem that most of the human remains in the chamber were early but the important thing is that the later closure incorporated evidence of what was in other respects a continuity of burial rite. These problems will be returned to, when mortuary practice is discussed as a separate issue, but the point to be made here is that the chambered cairns should not be viewed as having just been large, permanently open graves in which the dead were disposed of and thereafter forgotten about. As will be seen, mortuary practice was a long and intricate process which had associated with it activities which may or may not have been connected in the neolithic mind with either the body or memory of a particular person.

Now, tribes which are organised on a lineage basis – be they segmentary or chiefdoms – pay great heed to their ancestry since it is the genealogy incorporated in this which validates the existing social structure and the relative positions of the people within it. Death may be a source of passing personal grief at one level but at another the dead remain of importance to the living, providing them with a charter for existence which includes their continued right to a particular territory. In such a circumstance, therefore, it is not so much the burial of the dead that is under consideration as the housing of the ancestors – the one becoming the other – and, in this light, magnificent territorial markers containing human remains make a great deal of sense.

The subject of religion has now been broached – and a knowledge of tribes of the present and of the recent past can leave no doubt of the importance this would have had in the functioning of society in neolithic Orkney. Our view of this in such a remote period can only be expected to be partial and is best prefaced with a preliminary discussion of tribal religion in general in order to give background and a context for the evidence that exists.

At an analytical level religion has two basic functions, these having been elucidated by Malinowski and Durkheim, founding fathers of the social sciences. In the first place it acts to explain, and perhaps permit indirect power over, matters which are beyond man's everyday control and, in the second, it reinforces the social structure and the prescriptions and proscriptions of society on the temporal plane. Men make gods in their own image, the other world tends to mirror the society it belongs to, belief and practice supporting its various facets and religious activity being intensified at points of crisis. Religious beliefs among tribesmen would be expected to reflect the segmentary nature of their own society, to involve what is important in its structure and culture, and to find particular expression over matters of individual or communal concern. This is the case but, in practice, the exact form religion takes varies greatly between one tribe and another.

In a segmentary tribe the main emphasis of the society is at its lower level, where the structure is strongest: the autonomous territorial unit. As would be expected the main emphasis of religious belief is there too and, that aside, it is the level where most of the trials and tribulations of the population are felt. At a personal level there tends to be belief in such things as witchcraft, and the efficacy of both the spells of sorcerers and the spirits in fetish objects. Here, too, close kin may be plagued by the ghosts of the recently departed until they are laid to rest by propitiation, and frequently through an extended burial ritual and accompanying period of mourning. The latter is one aspect of what is loosely described as ancestor worship, this being a stage removed from simple genealogical appreciation in that the dead are seen as having a continued influence over the living. It is particularly associated with tribes with structures based on lineages – though not inevitably – and in a second form the dead are thought to join the spirit world from where – providing sufficient notice is taken of them – they support the interests of the group they are ancestral to while, at the same time, keeping an eye on the proprieties of their descendants. This belief can be seen to be effective at the level of the territorial unit and parallels to it are totemic spirits and nature spirits – though they need not be mutually exclusive. Even in a segmentary tribe the supernatural does tend to have higher entities which are concerned with less local issues but they are often vaguely perceived and for most purposes are not approached; they may even be considered to have an Olympian indifference to the joys they bestow and the sufferings they inflict on mankind. This is in keeping with the idea of autonomy of the basic territorial units; where there is ancestor worship the links between lineages are not stressed and where a greater god or spirit is called upon it may take on a strictly local persona.

In a chiefdom the local level of religious beliefs and practices is not done away with but is integrated in a non-divisive way into a system in which stress is placed on the upper parts of the supernatural hierarchy – and hence on the society as a whole and the positions of those who hold authority within it. There may, for example, be a great spirit or god who is held to have made the known world – and whose interest often thereafter ceased – and below that there might be a number of powerful entities who control things of great importance to the tribe as a whole – such as the sun, the moon, the fertility of the earth, and so on. In a tribe with ancestor worship the spirits of the dead may be considered to become incorporated within these greater supernatural beings and thus provide local sub-deities. The paramount chief is frequently thought to be in contact with the gods, through his priests, if not directly descended from them. He takes on their aura and is an intermediary in all that affects man most. Thus semi deified the important times of his life may be marked by great public ceremonies and he becomes the pivotal character in the building of great religious monuments, in the carrying out of rites involving the prolonged mobilisation of the whole people and the offering of splendid sacrifices.

It can clearly be seen how this would reinforce the status of the paramount chief, validating his authority in all matters, including his right to call on goods and services as he saw fit. It would also bind together his people at a tribal level, with cohesion resulting from the seeming resolution of matters of general concern, their involvement in centralised ceremonies, and their continual commitment to the support of a paramount head of the social structure within which they existed. As has been mentioned, however, tribal religion is as segmented and hierarchical as the society involved and similar mechanisms would exist at each level and within each group. In a society in which ancestor worship played a prominent part there might, therefore, be shrines or bone repositories for each division of geographically spread lineages. These, or shrines to totemic spirits, nature spirits, or lesser forms of the great deities would be the focus of ceremonies of their own. The interests of a particular subdivision within the tribe would thus be pursued at a local level through the person with most authority and, again, both his status and the identity of the group as a whole would be reinforced.

The chambered tombs and henges still in existence are thus just the skeletal remains of a religious subsystem of society which would have been of as vital importance to the whole as the linked ones of politics, economy and kinship. At a theoretical level these monuments can be imagined as having been the former sites of ceremonies, ritual, and great feasts but the question remains as to whether any light can be thrown on the religious beliefs and activities that existed in neolithic Orkney. The view is not total but there are three areas of research that offer particularly valuable insight.

Mortuary practice

It was obvious from the beginning that the human remains in the chamber at Isbister had not been subject to the sort of burial process familiar to our society. Bodies had not been taken in as such for there were no skeletons present – indeed, not a single instance was noted of any of the bones having been deposited while still articulated. At the same time there was distinct order, rather than chaos, and the picture, partly extrapolated, is of little piles containing a skull and other bones along the sides of the main chamber, skulls in the side cells and residual bones under, and perhaps on, the shelves of the end stalls. There is evidence of definite system and method here – no matter how foreign it might be to us. One possible clue, noted at the time of excavation, was that the discrete piles of bones in the main chamber may in some way have been the remains of individuals and, as has been mentioned, one of these was lifted separately in order that the idea could be tested.

There is also the clue that it was not bodies that were taken in, but bones, and when Judson Chesterman came to look at the human skeletal remains he found them to be bleached and weathered – in contrast to the animal bones which had also been in the chamber. Further, intensive analysis showed him that only parts of skeletons had been involved and that fragments of some of the bones were missing. Most of the individuals he was able to distinguish were diagnosed from only a dozen bones and fragments and a few from only one or two. In summary it is quite clear that the bodies of the dead had been excarnated – defleshed – outside the tomb before a selection of the skeletal remnants were transferred to the chamber.

It is quite possible that excarnation took place in the immediate vicinity of the tomb and this provides one potential explanation for the forecourt. It must be borne in mind that forecourts and similar delimited external areas are known to exist at other sites as well. Investigation of the forecourt at Isbister would have thrown no light on the hypothesis since it consists of bare rock. The actual defleshing of a body may be carried out in several different ways although the condition of the Isbister bones means that fire or anything akin to butchery can be excluded. The possibility of the bodies having been temporarily buried in sand or earth also seems unlikely because of the lack of a suitable location within a reasonable distance of the tomb. If, however, they had been simply laid out they would no doubt bear the marks of carnivores, such as dogs, and in the absence of any gnawing or cracking I personally favour the hypothesis that the dead were exposed on constructed platforms with excarnation being effected by decay, carrion-feeding birds, maggots, and the elements.

Questions that might be asked are how often deaths occurred

in the community, how long bodies were exposed – more particularly, whether it was for a specific period of time – and how the bones to be kept were selected. Both of the latter queries could be greatly illuminated by practical experiment but, in the present absence of this, archaeological evidence alone will have to suffice. On the basis of the number of corpses represented by the thousands of bones in the chamber of Isbister and the known span of its use it can be suggested that deaths at most would only have occurred within the community on average every six months and that there would therefore have been something like two excarnations a year. At the other end of the scale of possibility there would have been a death, and hence excarnation, every three years or so. It has been seen that the process lasted sufficiently long for the bones to become bleached and weathered but some ligaments may have survived since certain bones, such as those of the feet and of the neck closest to the skull, were over-represented. This would lead to the tentative conclusion that this stage of dealing with the body was considered finished when excarnation was completed but the evidence from Quanterness – where Chesterman found the same overall situation obtaining – suggests otherwise. There the bones in the chamber were *not* all in similar condition, some being in prime condition and others so weathered and broken as to be almost unidentifiable. It may be, therefore, that the timing of bones being taken into the chamber was not dictated by the stage of excarnation reached but rather that this happened on a specific, perhaps annual, occasion which might have been more of a public than a private affair. If a year is taken as a possible interval between the ceremonies then it can be imagined that the bodies of those who died early in this term would have been reduced to bones while the very recent dead would still be corpse-like. More evidence on this subject will be given below. The actual selection of bones from the remains of an individual seems to have been quite unsystematic and it is possible that it was rather negative in that all that could be chosen from was what remained after the natural agents of excarnation –

including perhaps gravity and wind – had taken their toll. It was, in any case, a token representation, there being little apparent effort to gather together and preserve every bone possible.

After the bones of one of the dead had been taken into the tomb they were initially placed in a pile along the walls of the main chamber. This is known to be the case because the example reserved to test the hypothesis proved to be the fractional remains of one person, a woman who died at the age of thirty-five (Fig. 23). There are admitted difficulties in corroborating this in other ways simply because burials were fractional and disarticulated but, nevertheless, Chesterman did show that while bones from the same individuals were found among those from the third and fourth stall there was no admixture between the two contexts. At this stage bones were considered and treated as being representative of a person, someone who was remembered by those that lived after. In time, however, their identity will have been forgotten – they will have simply become one of the ancestors – and this may in part explain the subsequent sorting of the piles, with skulls being placed in one context and the post-cranial bones in another. This was done with evident care, no matches having been noted between the bones in the main chamber and those in the third side cell and the fifth, shelved, stall. In citing this occurrence at Isbister a step has been made towards understanding the compartmentalisation of other tombs and the necessity of routes of access has been underlined.

The basics of the mortuary practice at Isbister have now been sketched but there remain a few loose ends to tie up. The foundation deposit under the floor of the fifth, shelved, stall, for example, consisted of 523 disarticulated bones and fragments from at least fifteen individuals. Clearly the bodies of these people had gone through the stages of excarnation and selection of bones but one is left to wonder whether what was found had

---

Fig. 23   The fractional excarnated burial of a woman aged 35 which was lifted separately from the chamber at Isbister

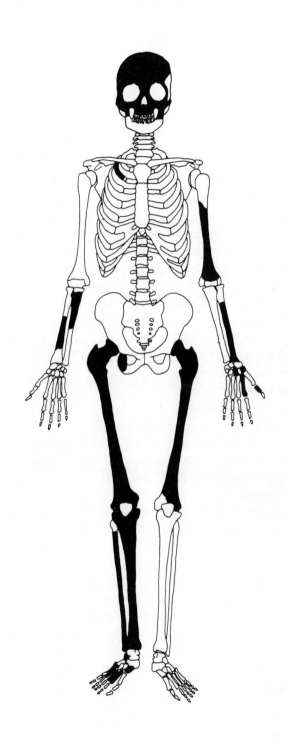

simply been stored pending the building of the tomb or whether it had been brought from a similar repository elsewhere. It is certainly interesting that only fragments of two skulls were included, since this may mean that the third stage of mortuary practice had been reached and it must be significant that one of the bones paired with another from *on top* of the floor of the same stall – the implication here being that other bones from the earlier deposit may have been present in the chamber. The closeness of the dates for the bones from the main chamber, side cell, shelved stall and foundation deposit – indistinguishable in radiocarbon terms – raises questions, too, about the speed with which the three stages of mortuary practice were gone through. It was obviously an affair which extended over decades or generations rather than centuries. One might also ponder the question of what happened to the mortal remains of members of the community who died between the period of intensive use of the chamber and the time it was infilled. It seems likely that they were excarnated – since the mixcd, disarticulated, weathered, fractional burials of up to eleven people were included half-way through the filling. It is equally obvious, however, that they were not generally placed in the chamber as there was only one bone of appropriate date, the others sampled being comparatively early. Perhaps the concept of the ancestors had ceased to include people who lived and died in the present time. If the ancestors became fixed and unalterable then little harm would be done in physically sealing their mortal remains. Whatever the reason it is clear that the process of excarnation and bone selection continued through to the Bronze Age for the putative cist to the north of the closed tomb contained fifty-nine bones belonging to three bodies. Though a millennium and a half of continuity can be shown in one sense, it is an unavoidable fact that the remains of the majority of the people who died in the neolithic period were not put into tombs but were disposed of in some other way – even while these monuments were still regarded as of great importance in other respects. Burial can again be seen to have been a subsidiary function and, as an extension of this, it seems possible that chambers may have been occasionally cleared out to varying degrees. It was the ancestral link which was vital and not the bones themselves.

Isbister has given us a rare insight, the undisturbed order of the bones being readily interpretable because of the knowledge that already existed of excarnation through the work of Judson Chesterman and Colin Renfrew at Quanterness. At the same time Quanterness goes to show how restricted our view becomes if the bones should have been crushed or otherwise disturbed for, even with foreknowledge of the possibility, the re-creation of any pattern that existed would be a formidable task. Given this, it might be asked whether there is any corroboratory evidence from other tombs in Orkney for the type of mortuary practice which has been revealed at Isbister. Fortunately, there is evidence for excarnation, bone selection, and subsequent sorting – and though a full catalogue is out of the question in the present context I would like to cite a few interesting and instructive examples.

At the Knowe of Yarso Callander and Grant noted in the 1930s that it was impossible to determine where a single body had been placed as 'no long bones occupied the relative positions of a skeleton either in a crouched or extended position'. However, the bone report made clear that the fractional disarticulated remains of one individual had been in the entrance passage, two in the first stall, one in the second, and eight in the third – where three skulls had been placed against the west wall, the other bones being post-cranial. In the fourth, terminal, stall there were, at ground level, seventeen skulls without their lower mandibles, cranium upwards, and facing towards the centre of the chamber while other bones said to have been 1 m above these were probably on a shelf. Callander and Grant also found the human bones in the thirteen-stalled chamber of Midhowe to have been particularly distributed. The remains of between two and four individuals were in each of the eastern sides of stalls 5–10 while in the west side of the eighth stall was an additional single deposit of bones. There are no exact details but individuals were said to have sometimes been represented only by a skull while in other instances there was a fractional excarnated burial – this being the excavators' interpretation, too. One such was described as having the long bones built up against the wall with the skull having been placed on top. The particular interest of this site, however, is that several of the burials are stated to have been crouched – one sitting – and there is photographic evidence of this. Now, Barry noted a skeleton in Quanterness, Traill-Burroughs one in Taversoe Tuick, and Clouston four in Unstan and, though these tombs – like several others – also had evidence of excarnation, it might be wondered whether there was one form of mortuary practice in the Orcadian Neolithic or two. I believe that such skeletons, discounting any late intrusions, are the product of incomplete excarnation, the individual having died only shortly before the customary time when the remains of the dead were taken into the chambers, regardless of their state of decay. This hypothesis is supported by the excavation evidence from the chamber of Quanterness for, in addition to the layer of clearly excarnated bones, there were four broadly contemporary pits, three of which were excavated and found to contain articulated human remains. What may be called the first had in it a few decayed pieces of a skull and a stain showing where a body had been. In the second the body had been disarranged after the dissolution of the softer parts with bones being broken and some removed: at this time the pit and its contents were subjected to fire and odd bones of two other individuals became incorporated. In the third pit there was only the lower part of a skeleton and here Chesterman concluded that inhumation had taken place following partial excarnation – while the ligamentous attachments were still intact. The upper part of the skeleton may well have been subsequently removed with the same heating of what remained and, certainly, some of the bones belonging to the body were found in the layer sealing the pit.

All this is very peculiar, though it is hoped that the general introduction to this chapter will have given some basis for understanding such practices. Having been so circumspect in keeping ethnographic parallels to the level of general observations I feel a little wary of giving one or two particular examples to illustrate the type of things that may have been happening. Though this will be done the reader must be aware that these are not intended in any way to be exact parallels, serving only to demonstrate that what is bizarre to one culture is quite normal to many others.

Exposure of the body is a form of disposal of the dead which is comparatively common. The Tibetans, for example, believe that it reunites the body with the air, and other methods of disposal used – such as casting the corpse into streams or lakes, burial in earth, or cremation – similarly unite it with the other elements: water, earth and fire. In Tibet even the bones are ground up with barley and fed to scavengers. The Mongols similarly abandon corpses in high places for wolves and eagles to consume and there is a saying among the Chinese of Central Asia that the eagle is the nomad's coffin. The custom is perhaps best known among the Zoroastrians of Persia and India (Parsees), large communities having specially constructed buildings – the towers of silence – where vultures make short work of mortal remains which would otherwise contaminate the purity of earth, fire and water (Pl. 20). Air burial was also one of the methods commonly used among the American Indians (Pl. 21) and I give as a special example the Choctaw of the Mississippi, detailed information on this tribe having been gathered together by John R. Swanton and published in 1931 under the auspices of the Smithsonian Institution in Washington.

In this tribe a scaffold was erected near the house of the dead person and the body was laid on it, covered by a blanket or bear skin, and out of the reach of dogs. The nearest female relatives would go each morning to weep through the seven or eight months necessary for the body to decay. When this had happened the 'bone picker', the principal official in their funeral ceremonies, appeared and informed the relatives of the deceased that the time had come for him to perform the last sacred duties of his office. These old men never trimmed the nails of their thumb, index and middle fingers, which accordingly grew to an astonishing length – sharp and almost hard as flint. With the relatives and friends he would march with great solemnity of countenance to the scaffold and, ascending, began his awful duty of picking off the flesh that still adhered to the bones, with loud groans and fearful grimaces, to which those below responded with cries and wailings. The flesh was then tied in a bundle and left on the scaffold to be burnt with it while the bones were gathered up, taken down, and placed in a specially prepared box. With more weeping and wailing the box containing the bones was then carried in procession to a specially constructed and consecrated 'bone house', one of which was to be found on the edge of every settlement. It should also be noted that these 'bone houses' were the venue for spring and autumn ceremonies connected with the dead and that when they were full the bones from those of an area were incorporated in a mound of cumulating size amid further ritual, wailing and feasting.

I have chosen as a second example the mortuary customs of the Lodagaa of West Africa, as detailed in J. Goody's book of 1962. These are concerned with neither excarnation nor collective burial but throw light on ghosts and the cult of the ancestors. The Lodagaa, in common with most of the world's people, believe that death is not the end but only the point at which the soul finally leaves the body. The problem for them is that initially it sits among the treetops enjoying the sexual, property and authority rights it had in life. Matters are also complicated by most deaths being put down to murder, witchcraft, or the malevolence of the ancestors, rather than natural causes. The spirit may materialise as a ghost and the bulk of the mortuary customs are concerned with settling the affairs of the dead person on earth so that he or she may become an ancestral spirit proper and travel on to the land of the dead. There are many stages of ritual purification during which the corpse and, particularly, the widow or widower are cleansed of contact and physical association. The kin are summoned, both those by direct descent and by marriage, and they all take part in extravagant ceremonies involving feasting, music, speeches and gift giving which, as well as propitiating the ghost, provide a pretext for his or her debts to be settled. The body itself is buried after the passage of three days – which are associated with grief, resignation, and final acceptance – but the persona of the individual is transferred to a temporary shrine, a length of wood, to which food and drink offerings continue to be made. The final transition from life to death comes only with a ceremony held after the first harvest following the burial. A proper anthropomorphic shrine is made and placed with those of the ancestors while the task of giving it offerings symbolically passes from the family to the lineage. The dead person's property has now been divided, the surviving spouse is free to choose another partner, and his or her former rights and duties have been distributed among the living. The ancestors, however, continue to have powers over the affairs of people and the way nature impinges upon them and are therefore worshipped through sacrifices, libations, gifts, prayers and respects. The Lodagaa have, for example, two post-harvest ceremonies – one general and the other for local descent groups – in which the ancestral shrines serve as a focus and births, marriages and deaths are also marked by performances connected with the ancestors. Any individual is obliged to offer the shrines part of goods he receives, whether by brideswealth, inheritance, farming, hunting, or wage labour, and the process is very much one of asking the ancestors for favours, thanking them, and hurriedly making forgotten offerings when some calamity falls. It is particularly interesting that no individual ancestor is remembered or worshipped for ever. As they become removed in time from the living they are succeeded, the genealogical link between distant and recent ancestors is progressively telescoped, and the shrines of the forgotten are gradually destroyed by wood-eating ants.

Table 4   Types of bird bones found at Isbister and the positions of their occurrence

TYPES OF BIRDS RESPRESENTED	Foundation	Chamber Use ST3	ST4	ST5	SC3	Closure	Hornwork	Unstrat/ Disturbed	Totals	%
Carrion-feeding birds of prey			+41							
White-tailed sea eagle	2	31	105	181	28	215	—	38	641	
Great black-backed and lesser gulls	1	6	1	14	2	1	1	3	29	95
Crow, rook and raven	—	6	5	5	—	—	—	3	19	
Nom carrion-feeding birds of prey										
Short-eared owl	—	3	3	—	—	3	—	—	10	2
Kestrel and goshawk	—	—	—	—	—	—	3	1	4	
Palatable species										
Woodcock, snipe, eider, goose, grouse, curlew, mallard, oyster-catcher, shag, puffin and little auk	—	—	3	—	3	2	9	5	22	3
									725	100

Totem and taboo

Human bones were not all that was found at Isbister for, as intimated, there were the multitudinous remains of birds, animals, fishes and seeds as well as a large number of manufactured objects of different types. To treat these as 'environmental remains' on the one hand and 'artefactual forms' on the other would be to seriously undervalue the importance of the evidence that exists. Before going on to their greater significance, it is necessary to give a brief account of what there was.

The bird bones certainly constituted the most extraordinary of the collections. Very few were from species which might have been taken for food; a staggering 97 per cent coming not just from birds of prey but, for the most part, from ones that will eat carrion (Table 4). The most singular fact of all is that 90 per cent of the bones of this type of bird belonged to one particular species – the magnificent white-tailed sea eagle – a bird which can live for over forty years and can have a wingspan exceeding 6 ft (Pl. 25). Odd bones of palatable species and non carrion-feeding birds of prey were recovered from both inside the chamber and in the material behind the northern hornwork but the bulk of the remains, those of carrion feeders, were within the tomb and had seemingly been taken in as complete carcasses (Fig. 24). The evidence for their disposition comes from the undisturbed parts of the chamber floor and this indicates that they had been laid both in the central stalls – where the excarnated burials were – and in greater numbers in the shelved end stall – where post-cranial bones had been put – but that few accompanied the skulls in the side chamber. There are problems attached to estimating the number of carcasses the bones represented both because of their fragility and because the analyst took them as a whole for this purpose rather than considering the birds as having been placed in discrete contexts. With this in mind I think that his estimate of five white-tailed sea eagles could comfortably be doubled or trebled while his other figures of two black-backed gulls, two crows (or rooks), a

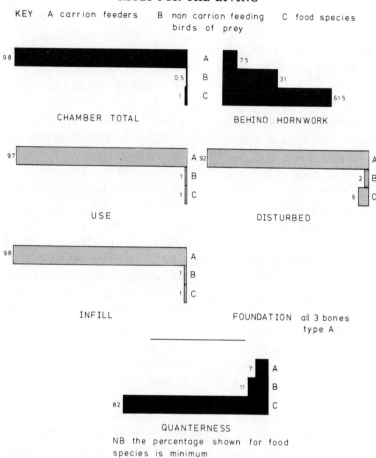

KEY A carrion feeders   B non carrion feeding   C food species
                             birds of prey

98 | A
0.5 | B
1 | C
CHAMBER TOTAL

7.5 | A
31 | B
61.5 | C
BEHIND HORNWORK

97 | A
1 | B
1 | C
USE

92 | A
2 | B
6 | C
DISTURBED

98 | A
1 | B
1 | C
INFILL

FOUNDATION all 3 bones
            type A

7 | A
11 | B
82 | C
QUANTERNESS
NB the percentage shown for food
species is minimum

Fig. 24 Percentages of bird bones of different categories at Isbister with Quanterness shown for comparison

raven, and two short-eared owls would have to be increased only slightly, if at all. This demonstrable emphasis on carrion-feeding birds of prey in a funerary context – and, more particularly, that of white-tailed sea eagles – is very interesting indeed. It predated the tomb, the foundation deposit having in it at least two white-tailed sea eagles' bones as well as one from a greater black-backed gull and, similarly, it continued through to the closure, an estimated 800 years later, the human bones in the infill being accompanied by up to eight eagle carcasses, as well as odd bones from other birds of prey and two possible food species. Taking the bones from disturbed contexts into account I would suggest that something like thirty-five carcasses of birds of prey had been involved in total and that two-thirds of these were white-tailed sea eagles.

Animal bones were also found in all the tomb contexts except the fill – where there was only a stray polished dog tooth which may have been part of a necklace. What is interesting, however, is that 61 per cent of the 1,000 bones and fragments recovered came from the excavated fraction of the material which had been banked behind the tomb and its hornworks in the third phase of construction. It would appear from the bone assemblage that young animals were selected, mostly cattle under eighteen months old but with some sheep or goats which were killed in their first year and a few similarly immature pigs, red deer and, apparently, otters. Butchery of the carcasses was limited to basic joint separation – there being an absence of any chopping – and the meat was put immediately out of the way of scavengers and the elements, without any of it having been cooked or eaten. Some was taken into the tomb but there was a distinct preference here for joints of mutton or goat meat (Fig. 25), particularly those of the legs, despite the fact that the majority of the carcasses available were of beef. The discrimination is both fascinating and important and while other species were less well represented it is possibly significant that no pig bones were definitely within the chamber while only a small proportion of those of deer and otters were outside it. The disposition of the meat in the chamber is again known only for the undisturbed part of the floor but the greater part appears to have been placed in the third and fourth stall since relatively few bones were under the shelf of the fifth stall and in the side cell. The number of animals killed and cut up is difficult to estimate since parts of the same carcass may have been placed in separate contexts and information is lacking for most of the area outside

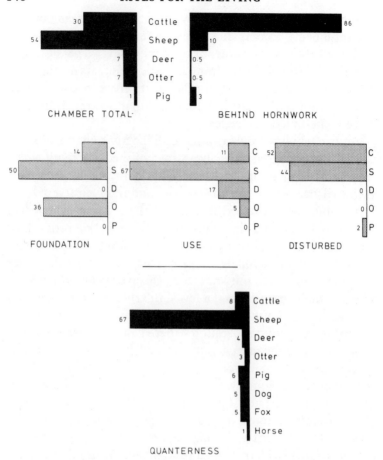

Fig. 25 Percentages of animal bones of different species at Isbister with Quanterness shown for comparison

the tomb. Clearly there were a great number for even just the bones recovered give minimum figures of sixteen cattle, and sixteen sheep or goats as well as four otters, a pig and a red deer. If the small area excavated was typical then further work on the material behind the tomb and hornworks would have increased the estimated number of cattle involved phenomenally.

The interior of the chamber would originally have been dark, damp and cold but the air would also have been thick with the stench of decay. The human bones were relatively clean when put in but the bird carcasses and joints of meat were left to rot where they were and the presence of hundreds of fish must also be taken into account. These are only really known about because the excavator had the presence of mind to collect material from the floor of the third, central, stall for sieving. Other parts of the chamber floor may have been similarly rich in such remains but even this one alone yielded 6,500 bones and fragments. The fish seem to have been taken in whole and, presumably, fresh. With one exception – a flatfish that may have weighed up to 2 kg – all were small, most being less than 500 g in weight and a few less than 100 g. Ninety-five per cent of the bones were accounted for by only a few varieties of fish – particularly sea scorpion or father lasher, rockling, and ballan and corkwing wrasse – and it is very noticeable that these are inshore species and, indeed, only two bones were tentatively identified as having come from a fish found in deeper waters. Simple hand recovery of fish bones is ineffective and it is not known whether there had been fish in either the foundation deposit or outside the tomb among the material behind the north hornwork. There were, however, two of the distinctive oral bones of wrasse with the eagles and human remains in the chamber fill and this may indicate that fish had originally accompanied them.

Shellfish were also present, though not as common as might be expected – only ninety shells in total were recovered, mostly those of limpets. Slightly less than half were in the chamber and it is interesting that twenty-one had had their apices removed and were in a discrete group under the shelf of the end stall while the remainder were in the central, third, stall. It is likely that the former were not deposited as shellfish, as such, but as specially collected shells. A carapace of a small edible crab was found preserved in the lower fill of the chamber and another accompanied the eagles and human remains, together with two limpet shells. Shells were also found in the material behind the northern hornwork and, again, two from limpets were with the late excarnated fractional burials in the supposed cist.

The things spoken of have relatively durable skeletons but any vegetable foodstuffs originally present would have simply rotted without trace unless they happened to be carbonised. Such remains were recovered by Ronald Simison from the floor material of the third, central, stall but it will be appreciated that these probably represent only a fraction of what was there originally and give no information about the presence of vegetable food in other contexts. It nevertheless remains of the greatest interest that the 303 seeds recovered give evidence for the inclusion of grain – predominantly barley – which had been processed, but still contained weed contaminants, and which was uncooked.

Pottery was by far the most obvious type of artefact deposited in the tomb – during its use as well as its excavation (Fig. 26). Directly opposite the entrance, against the western wall of the third, central, stall, were hundreds of sherds weighing 28.5 kg which came from at least forty-six different vessels. Half were distinctive bowls of Unstan form, the collars of most of which were highly decorated; the others were variable but included deep round-based bowls with knobs or lugs. Only one anomalous sherd came from a flat-bottomed vessel. The sheer mass of this pottery and its restricted distribution are interesting but so, too, is the fact that the vessels were only partially represented and that they were burnt, seemingly after they had been broken. This burning could not have taken place within the chamber for there was no evidence for it but whether it took place in the domestic hearth or within the tomb complex is a question that remains unresolved – though it might be noted that only three small and featureless sherds were found among the material behind the north hornwork. The process which the pottery went through seems to have been shared by two other less well-represented classes of artefact – bone pins and flints

---

Fig. 26   Unstan Ware from the chamber floor at Isbister

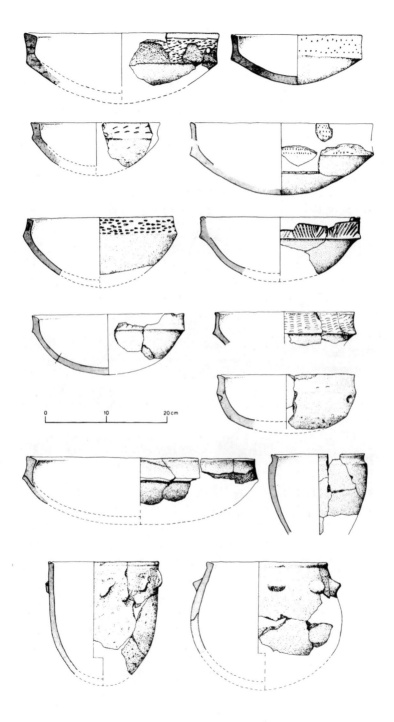

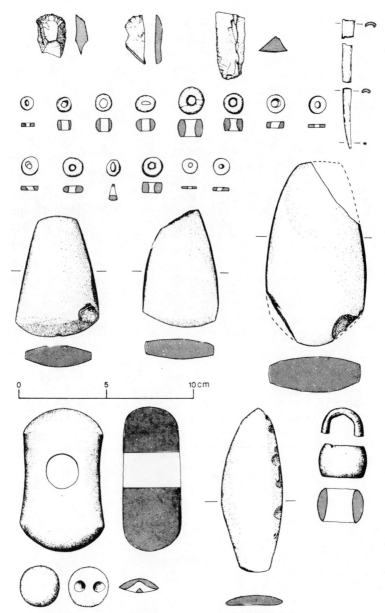

Fig. 27 Objects from the floor, chamber fill and outer scarcement at Isbister. From top left: flints; calcined bone pin; beads; stone axes; stone mace-head; pre-form of stone knife; jet ring; and jet button

(Fig. 27) – though the fact that most of the largely calcined remains of these were recovered through sieving leaves an uncertainty whether their distribution within the chamber was originally as limited.

The picture that is being built up is not just of birds of prey, foodstuffs, and artefacts having been deposited in or near the tomb but of their having been specially chosen according to context. Thus burnt and broken pots, pins and flints were taken into the chamber and were not generally in the material behind the northern hornwork while with what might be called crude stone artefacts the opposite was the case. The latter assemblage included nine beach pebbles which had been used as hammer-stones, two mattock-type implement blades, the tip of an ard share (a primitive plough share), a peck-handled 'club' – which had been rather damaged by secondary use as a hammer – and a peculiar, thin, handled piece of rectilinear flagstone (Fig. 28).

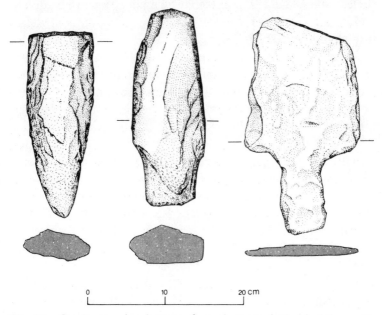

Fig. 28   Crude stone implements from the material behind the north hornwork at Isbister

In a third context, the chamber infill, there were a scatter of thirteen bone and shell beads and a polished dog's tooth – unassociated with the human remains, eagles and fish there. Finally, on the scarcement of the outer wall of the tomb front there were three polished stone axe heads, a magnificent mace head with a cylindrical perforation, a stone knife in the process of manufacture, a highly polished V-bored jet button, and half of a polished ring or pendant of the same material – representatives of the most treasured items of the age.

Before going on to an appreciation of the significance of all this it might be wondered whether the very clear situation obtaining at Isbister was in any way typical. Unfortunately the information from other tombs is comparatively deficient – either because they were badly excavated, because the contents of the chamber were found in a disordered state; or because the exterior was examined with insufficient care, if at all. Nevertheless several general points may be made. Meat from animals and, to a lesser extent, from fish and birds was commonly taken into chambers; Isbister alone provides evidence for vegetable foodstuffs. The types of animals present at Isbister were represented elsewhere and the limited evidence that exists corroborates the idea of their having been young and of butchery having been on the spot and rudimentary; at some tombs, however, charring of the bones indicates the meat to have been cooked. What is of special interest is that the type of meat taken preferentially into the chamber appears to have varied from one tomb to another. At Quanterness, Blackhammer, and the Knowe of Rowiegar it was mutton or goat, as at Isbister, but at Midhowe it was beef, and, at the Knowe of Ramsay and the Knowe of Yarso, venison. This shows clear discrimination, for the evidence from habitation sites indicates that cattle and sheep were kept in approximately equal numbers whereas there were few pigs and deer were of little importance in the economy. While the remains of fish, shellfish, and birds – including eagles – are known from several tombs the only reliable information available, in addition to that from Isbister, comes from the chamber of Quanterness and here again there are indications of discrimination. As at Isbister the fish bones, though few, were from relatively small fish which had generally been taken from inshore waters while those from the settlement of Knap of Howar prove that large fish were also being taken from further out to sea. Similarly, sea shells, rare at Isbister, were absent from Quanterness and yet occur in their tens of thousands on contemporary habitation sites. As for the birds present at Quanterness there are neither the birds of prey of Isbister nor the medium to heavy carcass-weight food species predominant in middens – virtually all the bones were from small song-birds.

Both the song-birds of Quanterness and the eagles and other birds of prey of Isbister are instances of the deliberate inclusion within tombs of distinct classes of organisms which are anomalous in that they are not obvious foodstuffs. Other instances that might be cited are the twenty-four dog skulls found near the chamber floor of Cuween; the dog skulls, or skeletons, found in each of the seven compartments of Burray; and the unusual occurrence of more than a dozen pairs of deer antlers inside the tiny Holm of Papa Westray North. Other examples may have gone undetected but there would seem to be evidence here of an unusual phenomenon, the exact expression of which differed from one tomb to another.

Here are examples of two pan-tribal institutions which showed systematic and distinguishing variation at a local level. The situation with the artefacts and their disposition seems to be entirely homogeneous but, again, it is one of definite discrimination. The things most commonly taken into chambers, as at Isbister, were burnt fragments of pottery vessels and flints, which are frequently calcined. The presence elsewhere of bone pins may have been generally overlooked, though there are examples. These things, moreover, tended to be placed in a group on the floor rather than being either distributed randomly or associated with any of the human remains. Valued objects, such as those found on the outer scarcement at Isbister, have also been found at several other tombs where they, similarly, were unburnt and were put in distinctive positions apart from the more mundane small finds and the osseous remains. Particularly favoured situations seem to have been either the inner or outer limits of the passage and the end compartments of stalled chambers. As at Isbister objects were placed only rarely in the intentional infilling of chambers – one notable and parallel example being a pendant and beads found in the upper passage of Taversoe Tuick. Finally, such artefacts as have been recovered from around tombs have tended to be coarse, functional, and rather ordinary. It is difficult to quantify artefacts but some idea of the selection involved is given by figures for the Knap of Howar where there were flints (75 per cent), pots (8 per cent), bone artefacts (7 per cent), pumice (6 per cent), crude stone objects (4 per cent) and polished stone implements (0.1 per cent). Without going into detail it can be seen that both pots and polished stone implements are rather over-represented in funerary contexts. There are indications, however, that preferences or prejudices operated at a yet more detailed level for while Unstan bowls, for example, formed half of the ceramic assemblage at Isbister and Unstan they constituted only a fifth of the vessels at the Knap of Howar.

But what does all this mean? The beads in the infill at Isbister may well have been lost and certain of the objects from behind the northern hornwork may have been included accidentally, having been used in building or in agriculture nearby. The same cannot be said for the bones found outside, the cache of precious objects, or anything within the chamber – their presence was quite intentional. These are the remains of sacrifices and ritual offerings – evidences of ceremonies and gatherings which had specific purposes and objectives in the minds of the tribesmen involved. Answers to such questions as what different types of ceremony there were, when they took place, what their aim was, and how many people were involved are largely beyond our present understanding – though a number of pointers do exist. *If* the joints of meat and birds placed in the stalls were associated with particular individuals then this may indicate a ceremony that took place when the excarnated remains were taken into the chamber. The real situation may have been more complex with meat being additionally or alternatively deposited with the ancestors that were fairly recent – though not necessarily newly dead – and the carcasses of birds of prey, offerings or not, being placed with or near the distant progenitors as represented by the heaped anonymous bones under, and perhaps on, the shelves of the end stalls. The taking in of bones may have been coincidental with annual ceremonies at times of the year when ancestors were felt to be particularly important – such as the beginning and end of the growing season – but there were possibly also occasions between times when the individual, family, or larger group was under particular stress. Much that could be put forward as interpretation is little more than guesswork but there is reason to believe that the tombs were ceremonial centres which housed the ancestors rather than simply being burial places. The reason why broken burnt pots, flints and pins were piled outside the entrance remains a mystery, though in some tribes the vessels used by the living are symbolically broken on their death. It is not known why so many fish were put in the tomb but these may have been the ancestors' share in the success of the living. It is difficult to imagine the reason for precious items having been placed on the outer scarcement, though they were certainly prestigious and represented a great sacrifice. Nevertheless, in all of these practices can be seen an emphasis on the role of the tomb as the repository of the ancestors, and not that the goods simply accompanied the corpse of an individual who thereafter ceased to be of significance to the living.

While only future research will provide more definite information about the timing and nature of ceremonies at such tombs there are two aspects about which Isbister has been particularly revealing. It has been seen that certain objects and, seemingly, foodstuffs were placed in quite strictly defined areas and this adds to the impression of a dominant pan-tribal cultural homogeneity. Within the tribe, however, the local unit was clearly of importance in the social structure – each built and used its own chambered tombs – and one might hope, therefore, to find traces of practices which served to reinforce this lower level of identity. One method used by tribesmen to distinguish individuals or groups takes the form of dietary restrictions, or taboos – in the widest sense of the word – the consumption of some foods being prohibited while that of others is favoured. Generally these are applied to particular circumstances, such as to parents before and after the birth of a child, to youths coming of age, or to mourners, but there is no reason why tribal subgroups should not have restrictions which differ in detail and thus serve to distinguish them. Whether the food was intended for the living or the dead matters not; the important fact is that not only are food restrictions apparent in the offerings taken into chambered cairns in neolithic Orkney but that they varied between one tomb and another.

Another, and perhaps better known, device used for distinguishing tribal subgroups is where they are identified with some aspect of the environment which becomes their emblem – their totem. Totemism may operate at the level of the individual or of the sexes but the phenomenon most commonly complements the divisions of a segmented social structure. Totems are usually animal or bird species though plants and inanimate objects may also be employed. To take American Indian examples, the Iowa clan totems were eagles, pigeons, wolves, bears, elks, beavers, buffaloes and snakes while those of the Moquis were deer, sand, water, bears, hares, tobacco plants, and reed grass. Sometimes a particular totem may take in several like species – such as the small bird totem of the Omahas – while on other occasions it may be only one part of an animal, bird, or plant. The attitude taken by the subgroup towards its totem varies from one society to another between veneration and simple acknowledgement depending on the need for identity reinforcement at different levels and the availability of other means for bringing this about. Where totems are very important they may be regarded as ancestral to the living – and to the title to their territory – and the living may be thought to become united with the totem on death. As with ancestral spirits in general they are seen as having an influence over man's well-being and behaviour towards them is regulated accordingly. Generally speaking they are not killed – except in structured situations – eaten, or used in any disrespectful way and they may be fed, animals and birds even being kept in captivity for the purpose. Should a member of a group find his totem animal or bird dead it is often buried with as much ceremony as if it were a human being. The totem may feature prominently in ritual connected with birth, puberty, marriage and death and the identification of a group with it may be such that they attempt to resemble it – by, for example, distinctive hair styles – and they may decorate their persons, possessions, and ritual centres with its likeness. The totem can be the ultimate symbol of a group, an easily understood expression of its identity for both members and outsiders. Given this, it is little wonder that such groups are often known by the name of their totems.

There are obvious impediments to our finding and recognising the remains of totems on archaeological sites. Some would not be preserved while others would be indistinguishable in our eyes from the general mass of things found – especially where there was any possibility of confusion with food. The white-tailed sea eagles and other birds of prey found at Isbister are thus quite exceptional since they defy alternative explanation and lead to the recognition of manifestations of the same phenomenon at other sites. With the totems the perceived identity of the groups which built the tombs is very closely approached indeed. It is even possible that here is an inkling of the names by which some were known.

Astronomer priests

It is possible that some of the activities at the chambered tombs were connected with the observation of the sun and the moon and, perhaps, with other celestial bodies. Apart from any religious overtones this may have had it would have provided a means of keeping a check on the passing years and on the seasons, perhaps dictating when certain ceremonies were to be held. The direct evidence for such knowledge is, at the moment, slight and concerns the orientation of the passages to the chambers. As David Fraser has pointed out most of these were built so as to open between ENE and due S. The effect of this would have been that the interior of each chamber would have been illuminated by the early morning sun during two periods of the year though it should be noted that as the orientations vary these periods would differ from tomb to tomb as would the interval between them. Thus, on purely theoretical grounds, one would expect the entrance passage at Isbister to be aligned with the early morning sun towards the beginning of April and again at some time towards mid September (Fig. 29). While the degree of conformity in passage orientation is striking there are a few known exceptions. Two are the upper passages of the two-storeyed tombs of Taversoe Tuick and Huntersquoy, and may perhaps be disregarded; two are unexplained, as yet; but the other three share a common orientation towards the southwest. One of these is Maes Howe, the chamber of which is illuminated by the setting sun on midwinter's day (Fig. 29).

After the chambered tombs there are the stone circles and these are of nationwide occurrence, more than 900 having been erected in a second phase of 'megalithic' building which started around 3000 BC. This has already been identified, in Orkney, with a conjectured chiefdom in which there was sufficient centralised authority – and reason – for two monuments on such a scale to be constructed. Evidence of another sort relating to these sites must now be taken into account, this being largely the work of one man, Alexander Thom, Emeritus Professor of Engineering Science at Oxford University. Over the last forty

Fig. 29   Alignments of the known entrances of Orkney tombs and the rising and setting positions of the sun (*after D. Fraser*)

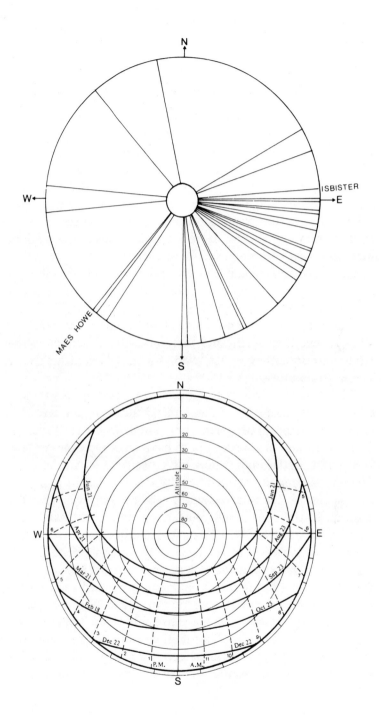

years Thom has measured a large number of stone circles and alignments in Britain and Brittany with a precision never before attempted. As a result of this, he has discovered three very exciting things – though it must be said that all are the subject of continued academic debate. In the first place standard units of measurement seem to have existed, a 'megalithic rod' (MR=2.07 m) being equal to two and a half 'megalithic yards' (MY=0.83 m). Second, some people at least in the later Neolithic and Bronze Age appear to have understood geometry for they were able to lay out stones in circles, flattened circles, ellipses, and egg shapes. Here integral numbers of standard measurements were employed for diameters and circumferences – as far as possible – and it should be noted that some of the work would have necessitated Pythagoras' triangles two millenniums before he was born. Third, and most spectacularly, Thom asserts that man had a knowledge of astronomy, from which he could derive true north, and that one of the functions of the circles – and standing stones – was as solar, lunar, planetary, or stellar observatories.

Thom's books on the subject are fascinating, though demanding reading, and I recommend them to the interested. While it is neither appropriate nor possible to give a full account of his work here it is necessary to have some brief idea of how and why celestial bodies may have been observed. As Euan MacKie has noted, before the invention of scientific instruments, just a few hundred years ago, the only way that the position of the sun, moon, planets or stars could have been noted accurately was by marking where they rose and set on the horizon. An observer seeing such an event could shift himself bodily until the occurrence took place over a distinctive natural feature; his point of observation could be marked and perhaps an alignment made by the erection of one or two foresights – such as standing stones – in order to establish the azimuth, as it is called, once and for all. This method works, at the simplistic level at which it has been explained, for the fixed stars as their points of rising and setting vary little over millenniums. True north could have been determined by bisecting the angle between the two azimuths for any one star and, given a knowledge of the solar calendar, they could have been used to give times of day. Thus, at midwinter Sirius would set at 2 a.m., Altair rise at 4 a.m., Capella set at 5.30 a.m., and Pollux set at 7 a.m. Observation of the sun is more complicated since its points of rising and setting shift with the time of year. At the equinoxes – 21 March and 21 September – it does rise exactly in the east and set exactly in the west and, as north was known and right angles could be made, it would have been possible to construct a calendar on the basis of this information alone. The evidence, however, points to greater sophistication still with the midsummer and midwinter solstices both having been noted. On midsummer day in Orkney the sun rises at its most northeasterly point and sets at its most northwesterly; on midwinter day it is above the horizon for the least time, rising at its southeasterly extreme and setting at its southwesterly. The time of the solstices – 21 June and 21 December – can thus be determined if azimuths are laid down on the days preceding them, since they are known to have occurred when these start returning in the opposite direction. In comparison to the sun the movements of the moon are extremely complex but Thom believes there is evidence that early man tracked the rising and setting points of this body too. Every month the moon's position on the horizon attains a maximum northerly value and, two weeks later, a minimum one further to the south – in a lunar month it goes through the same sort of process as the sun does in a year. The problem is that the rising and setting points vary between each month over a cycle of 18.61 years and, additionally, the position of the sun causes a wobble, or perturbation, which has a period of 173.3 days and which also affects the moon's course. It will be seen from this that the ability to mark the extreme rising and setting points of the moon is evidence of a sophisticated level of astronomical knowledge, the implementation of which would have taken years of observation. Such study of the moon would have given lunar months which could have been tied into the solar year since the most northerly risings and settings, the maxima, occur near the spring and autumn equinox. The total information available would also have been sufficient to permit the prediction of both lunar and solar eclipses.

In turning from a consideration of the subject at large to a discussion of the pertinent Orcadian monuments on their own it is unfortunately impossible to illustrate all of Thom's points. Both the Stones of Stenness and the Ring of Brodgar have now been surveyed accurately but information on the possible observation of the moon is almost totally limited to the latter and alignments with positions of the sun, planets, and stars have yet to be looked for. There can be no doubt that much information remains to be discovered and it should not be forgotten that single and grouped standing stones survive in forty-three separate locations in the isles as a whole.

The Stones of Stenness were probably originally twelve in number, each standing to a height of some 5.5 m. A striking feature of the two stones which survive *in situ* and entire is their angled tops and though this is a product of natural fracture planes in the sandstone it may nevertheless have been taken advantage of deliberately. Quite a large number of other standing stones exist or are known to have existed in the neighbourhood and some may well have been outliers of the Stones of Stenness though the proximity of the Ring of Brodgar makes for confusion. Graham Ritchie's recent excavations resulted in an accurate plan of the Stones of Stenness showing not just the surviving stones but also the position of the sockets that some of the others had once occupied (Fig. 30). Computer analysis based on the eight most accurately known positions indicated that the 'circle' had in reality been laid out as an ellipse which was oriented roughly true NNW and which had internal axes of 32.84 and 30.3 m. Further, the stones – each weighing about 10 tons – had been set with comparative precision at 30° intervals around the perimeter, the maximum error noted being 4.5°. Conversion of the measurements from this particular survey to

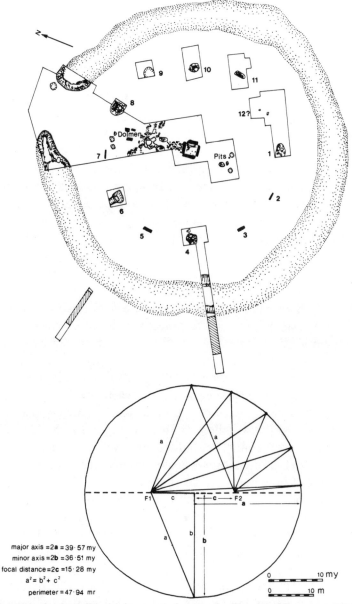

9

10

11

8

12?

Dolmen

7

1

Pits

6

2

5

4

3

major axis =2**a** = 39·57 my
minor axis =2**b** = 36·51 my
focal distance =2**c** =15·28 my
$a^2 = b^2 + c^2$
perimeter = 47·94 mr

F1   c   c   F2   a

a   b   b

0   10 my

0   10 m

Fig. 30 Graham Ritchie's excavations at the Stones of Stenness. The diagram below indicates the manner in which the stones may have been laid out (*after J.N.G. Ritchie & A. Thom*)

Thom's megalithic units does not give results which are immediately impressive. The major axis of the ellipse becomes 39.57 MY, the minor axis 36.51 MY, the focal distance (a measurement to be explained) 15.28 MY, and the perimeter 47.94 MR. Implicit in Thom's hypothesis, however, is that there would frequently have been difficulty and compromise in obtaining radii and perimeters which were both of an integral number of units. Here the perimeter is very close to 48 MR, which means that the intention may have been to set the centres of the twelve stones involved 4 MR apart. There is the further point that the other measurements, if taken as integral numbers, are the sides of a Pythagoras' triangle (13:12:5) and such measurements seem to have been particularly favoured. The ultimate perimeter may have been given by trial and error but here, as elsewhere, the people were capable of drawing an ellipse on the ground. The simplest method of achieving one for the Stones of Stenness would have been to put in two pegs 15.28 MY apart (the focal distance) which had a rope attached to them 39.57 MY long, excluding knots (the major axis). If a stake was inserted into the loop, drawn tight, and dragged around it would describe an ellipse having a minor axis of 36.51 MY and a perimeter of almost exactly 48 MR (Fig. 30).

The surviving stones of the great Ring of Brodgar are an imposing sight, the tallest of them being 5.6 m high. Colin Renfrew's excavations there added greatly to our understanding of the ditch but did not investigate the encircled interior or give any idea of how many stones there had originally been in the circle – though this is usually quoted as sixty. The accurate survey that exists is owed to Thom (Fig. 31) who found the line of the centre of the existing stones and stumps to fit best to a circle with a diameter of 103.833 ± 0.134 m. He considers this firmly supports his theory of measurement, a diameter of 125 MY (103.75 m) having been chosen in order to give a circumference of 157.08 MR – which is very nearly integral. Thom seems to subscribe to the idea of there having been sixty stones, saying that they were meant to be 6° apart, starting from

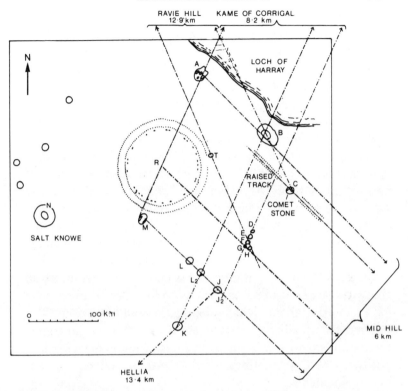

Fig. 31   The Ring of Brodgar showing possible lunar alignments
(*after A. Thom*)

geographical north. If one sketches the missing stones into his
plan, however, in its western half – where the circle is best
preserved – one finds fifteen in the south-western quadrant and
sixteen in the north-western – giving an estimated total of
between sixty-one and sixty-three. Were it the latter then the
intention may have been to set them 2.5 MR apart, the exact
figure for this number being 2.49 MR. It is of further interest
that Thom sees the average width of the surrounding ditch top
as having been 5 MR, the distance between it and the stones
being 1.5 MR.

In his earliest publication of the site Alexander Thom

mentions there being several time/azimuth sets for the sun as seen from the centre of the circle, though no details of these seem to be published. His main interest in Brodgar and its outlying mounds and standing stones has focused on its apparent use as a lunar observatory for, in his own words: 'Here, as in no other place, there are enough remains to prove conclusively that the movements of the moon were being fully observed.' The fact of the matter is that there are only four fixed points in the complex cycle of the moon and Thom has found between one and four alignments for each which coincide with distinct parts of the horizon. At its extreme major standstill the moon would have risen over a slope on the Kame of Corrigal and set in a small dip near Ravie Hill. Some nine years later, at the extreme minor standstill, it would have risen in a small clean-cut notch on Mid Hill and set on the cliffs at Hellia (Fig. 32). Apart from the understanding this supposes it also points to an ability to carry out observations over a long period in order to get exact azimuths on which alignments could be set up. The markers are usually considered to be Bronze Age, because most are mounds, but the original location of the henge-ring in a position where such sitings could be made is unlikely to have been coincidental.

Thom, quite rightly, views his findings in a broad perspective, taking uniform measurements and a knowledge of geometry and astronomy as part of the general culture of both Britain and Brittany. He has gone further in stating that such knowledge could only have been brought about, refined, put into action, and transmitted from generation to generation, if there had been people whose specific remit it was – what might be called astronomer priests – and I, too, would subscribe to this theory. Is the possession of such scientific knowledge and the possible existence of 'astronomer priests' consistent with the idea of a tribal social organisation? I think it is – and, particularly, in the case of a chiefdom. Here the flow of economic surpluses is used partly to support the chiefs and especially the paramount one together with his entourage of noble kin and

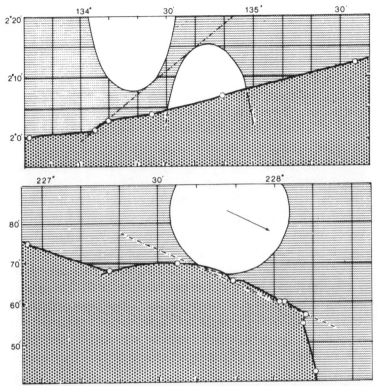

Fig. 32 The moon at the minor standstill as seen from Brodgar rising on Mid Hill and setting on the cliffs at Hellia (*after A. Thom*)

executive and ceremonial officials – as far as these can be differentiated. The latter may be called priests and their offices are very important in that the liaison of the paramount chief with the high gods is seen as vital for the good of the tribe – and, in reality, is as vital for his position. As has been previously discussed this picture of paramount chiefs, high gods, and priests is completed in the tribal world by grand centralised ceremonies which often take place at great monuments, these being both product and reinforcement of the chief's authority.

It is worth illustrating this with a concrete example from the many which exist and could be cited: here is one from Hawaii, summarised by Marshall D. Sahlins:

> . . . above and beyond the cult of lower levels was a religion of tribal dimensions, devoted to gods of universal compass – Kane, Ku, Lono and Kanaloa especially. The pivotal human figures in this sphere of culture were ruling chiefs and high priests, and the central places of worship were public monuments (*heiau*), stone platforms on which were situated various cult houses and god images.
>
> The life-crisis rites of high-ranking chiefs were public events, marked by ceremonies at main temple-platforms in the chiefdom. Apart from their divine descent, ruling chiefs apparently had special relationships to powerful guardian gods (*akua*) . . . The principal temples of a chiefdom were houses of Ku and Lono particularly: Ku, 'the god of war and chiefs', and Lono, god of peaceful pursuits, associated with agriculture and fertility. Ku and Lono (at least) had special orders of priesthood devoted to them. These priests presided over the Ku- and Lono-rituals at the greater temples, but shared their privileges with paramount chiefs, to whom fell the right and the obligation to intone certain very sacred prayers.
>
> A lunar month had specified days tabu to Kane, Ku, and other gods, and on these sabbaths religious observance was thus transposed to the tribal level. Periodically, too, and especially when contemplating war, a paramount chief would decide to build a special temple to Ku . . . a process involving human sacrifices, exorbitant offerings, prolonged ceremonies, and the mobilization of the whole people. The whole people also were annually mobilized – or rather immobilized by a tabu on ordinary work – for the great *Makahiki*, a harvest and renewal ceremony of many weeks' duration (four months, according to most authorities). Here Lono was the central supernatural; his image was carried in procession around an island chiefdom, watching games and sport in every district and collecting from each place a major first-fruits offering.

But the ruling chief was again the central mortal – sharing the food gifts to Lono, incidentally, with the priests.

We have then the conditions. There is also some slight evidence from Stenness in that the heads and hooves of animals were found in the ditch while a square central feature had been the scene of burning in which at least animal bones, or meat, and sherds had been involved. There are countless examples of tribesmen taking an interest in the sky and in the heavenly bodies in it, couched largely in religious terms, but is there reason to believe that any such people could have been proficient in the intricacies of astronomy without their having imported experts or knowledge from some advanced culture? One example is sufficient to decide this point and that is the Hopi pueblo Indians of the American Southwest for these had a calendar based on the position of the rising sun on the horizon with which their ceremonial and agricultural activities were linked. Daryll Forde may be quoted here, illustrating the point being made by a diagram in which Renfrew juxtaposed the Hopi calendar with Thom's histogram of notable alignments with the rising and setting sun and moon as seen from stone circles (Fig. 33):

The agricultural season opens in February with the clearing of the fields and ends with the last days of September when the last corn and beans are gathered in. Although the condition of the weather and the season determine the precise time of various agricultural operations, each stage is also anticipated and regulated according to a precise calendar. This calendar, which serves also to determine the dates of the many ceremonies, is provided by the daily shift in the position of sunrise on the horizon. The smallest irregularities on the southern sky-line are well known, and the more significant within the sun's path, probably some twenty or more, are named with reference either to their form, to ceremonial events, or to agricultural operations which fall due when the

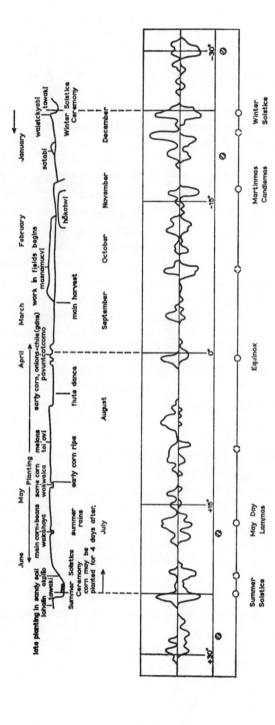

Fig. 33 The skyline as it served the Hopi Indians for a calendar with below, for comparison, Thom's notable alignments with the rising and setting sun and moon as seen from stone circles (*after C. Renfrew*)

O ☽ Sun's declination at 16 calendar dates

⊘ Moon at 4 limiting declinations

sun rises immediately behind them . . . The daily observation of these positions of sunrise is the duty of a religious official, the Sun Watcher, who forewarns the people of important dates and announces them in due course; he also keeps tally on a notched stick.

(D. Forde, *Habitat, Economy and Society*, 1934)

The interesting thing is that Hopi society was essentially egalitarian. There is no reason why the sort of knowledge Thom has pointed to could not have been created and used within the favourable conditions of a series of chiefdoms, indeed, it may have its roots in earlier, and simpler, social organisations. In this, as in the case of the tombs, there is no need to look upon our own prehistory as being in some way culturally dependent upon the outside. In these last two chapters I have used the new information from Isbister and have, by incorporating the opinions of others, arrived at what I hope is a coherent and plausible account of the independent social organisation that existed in just one area in one epoch – Orkney in the neolithic period.

5 · The People of the Tombs

Structure and dynamics of a dead population

The collection of neolithic human bones recovered from the tomb of Isbister was formidable. There were some 16,000, mostly fragments, and the problem of their analysis was compounded by the facts that only a selection of the bones belonging to any one corpse had been included and that the skeletal material as a whole had become intermixed to a certain extent both in antiquity and in consequence of the excavations. It does not require any specialist knowledge to appreciate the difficulty of trying to estimate the number of individuals involved, let alone their sexes and ages, and the results achieved by Judson T. Chesterman are testimony to both his expertise and perseverance. It is doubly fortunate in that it was the same expert who analysed the 13,500 fragmentary human bones which came from the excavations at Quanterness. Taken together, the two assemblages give an insight which is of unprecedented quality not just for Orkney, or for the Neolithic, but for prehistory in general. Other human remains of the neolithic period are known from Orkney, from some of the other excavated tombs and also from Skara Brae, but the main emphasis here will be on the Isbister/Quanterness assemblages because of the quantities involved and the standard of their recovery and analysis.

The first question to be asked was how many corpses the bones found at Isbister and Quanterness represented. The type of mortuary practice involved makes this difficult to answer but the situation was akin to that of estimating the number of animals, fish, or birds present in a midden where their bones are intermixed and the skeletal remains of any one organism incomplete. At its simplest the method used is to sort the bones into types; only specific numbers of each type are present in any one skeleton and that which is most frequent in the collection will therefore give a *minimum number of individuals*. This process is capable of certain refinements – bones from different contexts being treated separately and factors such as age and sex being taken into consideration. On this basis Chesterman estimated that at Isbister there were bones from fifteen individuals in the foundation deposit under the slab floor of the shelved end stall; 312 on the chamber floor; eleven in the infill; one among the material behind the north hornwork; and three in the 'megalithic cist'. This gives a total figure of 342 which, given the conditions, must be on the low side, but which he feels to be substantially correct. While the numbers of individuals in the different contexts are of interest, for the purposes of this chapter the human remains from Isbister will be treated as a single group since, with the exception of the three individuals represented in the supposed cist, they are all of neolithic date. Using the same method for the bones from Quanterness Chesterman arrived at a minimum number of 157 individuals. Only part of the chamber had been excavated, however, and Renfrew's extrapolated figure of 394 gives a clearer idea of the total number of bodies that would have been represented. These are large numbers and, in themselves, are in keeping with the idea of such tombs having been used to house the dead of particular communities over many generations.

A second problem was to determine the age of death of the individuals. Our bones change from the time we are born – in fact from before we are born – and skeletal remains from archaeological sites can therefore be examined from the point of view of the stage reached. In childhood, for instance, there is the eruption of milk and then permanent teeth; in juveniles the ends of the long bones fuse; and in middle and old age there is closure of the cranial sutures together with structural alterations in certain bones. The ageing of bones by these and similar indices must not be taken to be exact and, in any case, what is determined is biological age – rather than real age – and, as is well known, decrepitude sets in early under hard, primitive conditions. This having been said, 24 of the individuals at Isbister died in infancy (0–2 years); 70 as children (2–12 years); 63 as teenagers (13–19 years); and 185 as adults (20 years or more). The figures for Quanterness were comparable, there being 10 infants, 26 children, 36 teenagers, and 85 adults among the 157 bodies identified. One can see that there was a huge number of deaths at an early age, a matter for further discussion at a later point.

The age of death again indicates that the chambers of these tombs were not reserved for a selected population and this impression is further reinforced by a third factor determined for the individuals from their bones – their sex. This is practically impossible to ascertain for infants and children but particularly with the onset of puberty certain differences do appear in the bones of males and females. Females have, for example, differently shaped pelvises, sharper upper rims to the eye sockets, and slighter muscle attachments. Out of the 179 teenagers and adults at Isbister 80 proved to be males and 39 females, the discrepancy probably being due to the 60 that remained unsexed. Certainly, in the case of Quanterness the figures were much closer, 32 males being identified and 27 females.

Demography – or the study of population structure and dynamics – uses, among others, those indices which have been determined for the collections of human bones from Isbister and Quanterness: size of population, age structure, and sex ratio. This is a branch of the social sciences, heavily dependent on statistics, which, in the normal course of events, relies on intricate and exact information such as that gathered in our own decennial census. The same principles can, however, be applied to information of a lesser order such as that gleaned from living tribes by anthropologists and that taken from past records, not collected for the purpose, by historical demographers. When I was working on the information from Isbister it occurred to me that the information derived from the skeletal material might be put to a similar use. It seemed an opportunity not to be missed and, working from first principles, I devised means of examining the structure of the neolithic population of Orkney. Since then I have discovered (I hope to the confusion of my critics as much as to myself) that just such a sub-discipline – palaeo-demography – has existed since the beginning of this century, that the human bones from Isbister were an unprecedented sample for the purpose, and that the work I had done independently was perfectly in order. The foremost exponents of the subject internationally – G.Y. Acsádi and J. Nemeskeri in Budapest, Fekri Hassan in Washington, and Kenneth Weiss in Michigan – published major synoptic works in the 1970s and the opportunity will be taken of introducing some of their results in this book. Since the principles and workings involved would rather overburden a chapter such as this I have simplified the presentation and will leave it to those interested in a greater level of detail to consult the monographs on Isbister and Quanterness and the works of the aforementioned authors.

There are problems which it would be unwise to ignore, e.g. it is necessary to assume that the remains studied are representative of the population of the times. There has been the difficulty with collections in general that the bones of the young either have not been recovered or have not survived. It may also be that only the dead of a particular status, age, sex, family or whatever were buried in one place. I think that there are reasonable grounds to consider that the bones in chambered tombs such as Isbister represent an accurate cross-section of the population – with the exception stated below – even while accepting that at times remains were disposed of in alternative ways. Second, one has to feel confident that the data relating to age and sex are accurate. Though Chesterman's expertise can be relied on, it is nevertheless necessary to take account of three important limiting factors here. One is that the mortuary practice indicated made analysis difficult and less certain, numbers used for statistical purposes having often to be extrapolated; a second is that ages and sexes given cannot be regarded as absolutely accurate; and the third is that it is biological age which is determined and not actual age. Finally, one has to assume that the population was stable, birth and death rates neither increasing nor decreasing, and any immigration being balanced by emigration. This is not as far-fetched as it sounds for, as will be seen, human populations – like animal ones – regulate themselves, significant alterations occurring only as a result of major influences such as the Neolithic and Industrial Revolutions. It might be thought that a lack of knowledge of the exact population of neolithic Orkney or of the Isbister or Quanterness community at any one time would also be a problem but this is not so. It is interesting to estimate such figures – as has been done – but the analysis attempted here takes a standard unit of population, be it 100 or 1,000, and is unaffected by the total population that existed. For this reason, and because Isbister is the site for which the most detailed information is available, I will be talking about an *Isbister type population* and generalising from it to describe the Orkney neolithic population, rather than considering the population of the Isbister community specifically. The problems of palaeodemography relating to Isbister and Quanterness have been stated and there is no doubt that they affect the accuracy of the findings. At the same time it is my opinion that it is the prehistorian's business to do the best he can with the information available.

The ages of death of the individuals whose bones were found at Isbister have already been given in a crude form. The information derived by Chesterman, when properly weighted, will however give a much more precise idea – the histogram (Fig. 34) shows this for a notional Isbister type population of 1,000. Although it is not intended to present the information from Quanterness in the same detail it may be noted in passing that the equivalent histogram would be very similar in shape. One can see that – in striking contrast to a modern population – there was a high incidence of death in the early years of life, that this slackened between the ages of ten and fifteen, but that most people who survived puberty died before they were thirty, comparatively few living on even to the age of fifty. It is cer-

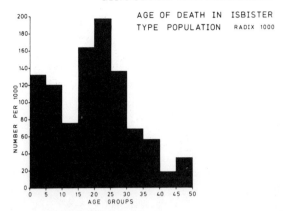

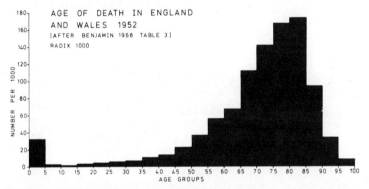

Fig. 34 Age of death in an Isbister type population contrasted with that in a modern population

tainly a grim picture, bringing to mind Hobbes' phrase that early man's life was 'poore, nasty, brutish, and short'.

When a policy is taken out on someone's life in these days the company involved consults actuarial figures – life tables – as the life-expectancy of the person concerned, at their particular age, can be calculated from these. In a life-table a notional number of births is taken for a given year – say, 1,000 – and the rate at which these individuals die over time is plotted. It is possible to construct such a table for an Isbister type population and it gives another view of the situation (Table 5). Before going on to

Table 5   Abridged life-tables for an Isbister type population and a modern population

| | Isbister type | | England & Wales 1952 | |
Age	Survivors	Deaths	Survivors	Deaths
0	1000	132	1000	32
5	868	120	968	2
10	748	76	965	2
15	672	164	963	3
20	508	197	960	5
25	311	136	955	5
30	176	68	950	7
35	108	56	943	9
40	52	18	934	13
45	34	34	921	22
50	0		899	36
55			863	55
60			808	80
65			728	111
70			617	142
75			474	167
80			307	173
85			134	93
90			41	8
95			8	8
100			0	

this, however, a rather specific instance must be cited and that is the infant mortality rate. This is defined as the deaths of infants under one year of age per 1,000 live births. In a civilised society with advanced hygiene and medical care this will be low whereas in primitive conditions it will be relatively high. The infant mortality rate that can be arrived at for the bones from Isbister of 49 per 1,000 births is clearly too low for the type of population involved; for pre-industrial groups, including pre- and post-contact primitives, and medieval and classical agricultural populations, Weiss gives a range of between 100 and 400 per 1,000. Although not the case at Isbister, Renfrew noted for Quanterness that babies dying before the age of eight months had seemingly been excluded from the chamber. In many primitive societies a child is not seen as a human being in its own right until a certain age has been reached or a particular *rite de passage* gone through. This, together with population control – as described below – can probably be taken to account for the phenomenon but it must be appreciated that direct evidence is lacking for a number of children who died, by one means or another, shortly after – or even before – birth.

Table 6   Life-expectancy in an Isbister type population

Age attained	Average life expectation	Average age expectancy
0	19yrs 11m	19yrs 11m
5	17yrs 6m	22yrs 6m
10	14yrs 11m	24yrs 11m
15	11yrs 4m	26yrs 4m
20	9yrs 2m	29yrs 2m
25	8yrs 5m	33yrs 5m
30	8yrs	38yrs
35	6yrs 6m	41yrs 6m
40	5yrs 9m	45yrs 9m
45	2yrs 6m	47yrs 6m

While bearing this discrepancy in mind it is still possible to use the life-table calculated in order to give an idea of life-expectancies in an Isbister type population at various ages. It can be seen from Table 6 that even if a child survived its initial months it could only be expected to live about 20 years – as an average. Colin Renfrew's estimate for Quanterness was 20–5. Similarly, those that survived their adolescence had then, on average, a life-expectancy of only some 9 years. Using the same modern population for comparison the contrast is again clear. The expectation of life at birth according to the 1952 life-table for England and Wales was 67.06 years for males and 72.35 years for females. At the age of 20 life-expectancy was 50.12 and 54.83 years respectively.

The reader may view the statistics obtained so far from the

Isbister and Quanterness human bones with scepticism. The picture offered is so unfamiliar that one might reasonably wonder whether there is any truth in it at all. However, in terms of the totality of man's existence on earth, it is our own demographic structure that is unusual. This can be readily demonstrated by Table 7 – originally compiled by Kenneth Weiss – in which the life-expectancy at birth is given for various prehistoric, historic and recent populations. It can be seen from this that an average lifespan of 20 years or so is quite in keeping with the figures for populations prior to, or remaining untouched by, the Industrial Revolution and modern medicine. It is, perhaps, a little on the low side but it must be borne in mind that an Isbister type population would have lived under more limiting natural conditions than most of the others examined, given Orkney's northerly position.

Table 7   Life-expectancy in various cultural groups (*after K. Weiss*)

Cultural group	*General range of life-expectancy at birth*
Australopithecines	about 15
Neanderthals	about 18
Hunter-gatherers to neolithic	19–25
Proto-agricultural	20–7
Living primitives	22–9
Classical and medieval	22–9
Sweden 1780	38
UK 1861	43
Guatemala 1893	24
Sweden 1903	54
Sweden 1960	73

To say that the average life-expectancy was around 20 years is one thing but some individuals would have lived longer, just as others would have died earlier. What is really required is an idea

Fig. 35   Age pyramid for an Isbister type population contrasted with one for a developed and an underdeveloped country

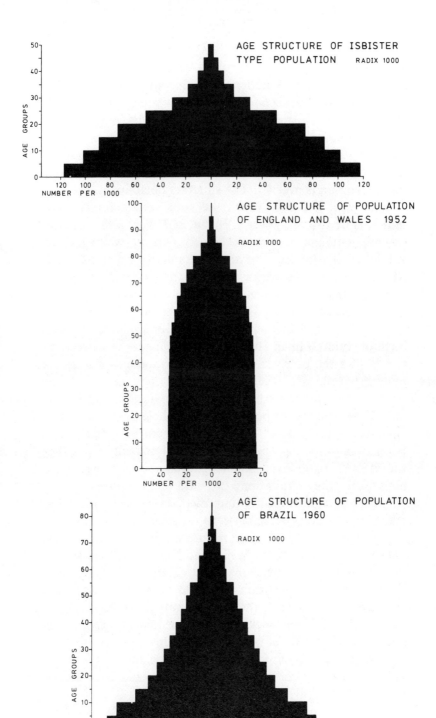

AGE STRUCTURE OF ISBISTER
TYPE POPULATION   RADIX 1000

AGE STRUCTURE OF POPULATION
OF ENGLAND AND WALES 1952

RADIX 1000

AGE STRUCTURE OF POPULATION
OF BRAZIL 1960

RADIX 1000

of the age structure that existed in a *living* Isbister type population and this the information available will provide (Fig. 35).
The resulting age pyramid brings out how young the population
would have been: those under 20 would have outnumbered
those over 20 by 3 to 1 and only 1.5 per cent of the people living
would have been over 40. In a modern population those under
20 are outnumbered 3 to 1 by those over 20 and 45 per cent of
the population is over 40! The situation obtaining in neolithic
Orkney was, however, much the same as that for any pre-
industrialised society, past or living, and even in the modern-
day population of an underdeveloped country – where an individual *may* live longer – the young are still in the majority. A lot
of children are necessary for the population to replace itself – so
many die before the age at which they can breed.

With the last comment I have gone from mortality to fertility,
relating the two. However, before going on to think about the
birth of children in an Isbister type population it is necessary
to consider the potential availability of mothers. The age of
puberty in primitive societies in general is fifteen and the figures
used to construct the Isbister type age pyramid indicate that
only 38 per cent of the population as a whole would have been
over that age. Some of this sexually mature portion of the
population would have been women – but not half. There is no
way of knowing how well or badly girls fared in comparison with
boys during the years of immaturity but the evidence of age for
sexed bones indicates that women died, on average, earlier than
males, most deaths being between the ages of 15 and 24. This
might strike us as odd, females in our own society tending to live
longer than males but, as Acsádi and Nemeskeri have shown,
this phenomenon is found in almost all pre-industrial populations from the palaeolithic period to the present day. The
apparent reason for it is the toll taken by the strains of preg-
nancy, childbirth and suckling where medical care is primitive
and where the health of women is worn down by poor diet and
the exacting nature of their traditional work. In his calculations
Hassan assumes that one in ten women would have died in

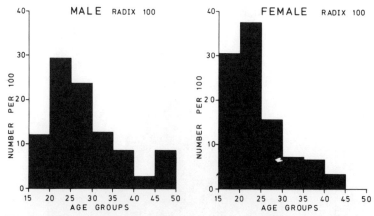

Fig. 36 Comparative ages of death in men and women over 15 in an Isbister type population

childbirth – while others have put it as high as one in five – and though the evidence from Isbister is weak an apparent jump in female mortality between the 10–14 and 15–19 age brackets probably reflects the onset of childbearing.

If it is assumed that an equal number of males and females survived to the age of puberty then the age of those dying over the age of 15 at Isbister (Fig. 36) permits the construction of a sexed life-table for the portion of the population which was capable of reproduction (Table 8). The important point might

Table 8   Abridged life-table for those having reached their fifteenth birthday in an Isbister type population

	Males		Females	
Age	*Survivors*	*Deaths*	*Survivors*	*Deaths*
15	100	12	100	31
20	88	30	69	37
25	58	26	32	15
30	31	13	17	7
35	19	8	10	7
40	11	3	3	3
45	8	8	0	
50	0			

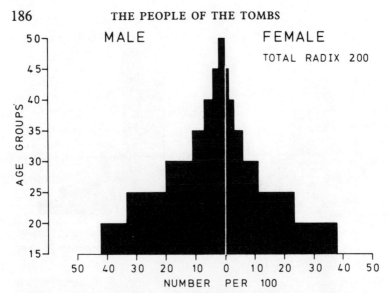

Fig. 37 Age pyramid for the sexually mature in an Isbister type population

be noted in passing that it is possible to calculate from this that, while male life-expectancy at 15 was just over 13 years, a girl arriving at puberty could, on average, expect to live only a further 9 years. The sexed life-table also makes it possible to construct an age pyramid which gives insight into the proportions of men and women there would have been in any age group (Fig. 37). If the sexes were equally balanced at 15 then by 20 there would have been three males for every two females and, by 30, two men for every woman. Above the age of 40 men, seemingly, outnumbered women by as many as seven to one. It is very important to note that only 40.58 per cent of the sexually mature population would have been women.

There are now several significant statistics at our disposal. It is possible to work out from the full life-table that 50.26 births would be required every year in order to maintain a stable Isbister type population of 1,000. Among such a population 383.4 would be sexually mature and of these 155.58 would be females of childbearing age. It would therefore have been necessary for these potential mothers to have had, on average, a child every 3.1 years. Further, if the average breeding span of a female was 9.05 years then the average number of children a woman had in her lifetime was 2.92. This immediately strikes one as a small number – but it is viable. If, over a certain area of neolithic Orkney, there were 1,000 births in a particular year then fifteen years later 672 of this number would have survived. If half were female – 336 – and each had in her lifetime 2.92 children they would in total have 981 – this, given the material, being an almost exact replacement of the number of babies from which their group survived.

It was assumed at the beginning that the Isbister type population studied was a stable one and that, over a period of time, generations were capable of exactly replacing themselves. Statistics derived solely from the human bones have now shown this to be so. At 50 births a year for each 1,000 people alive there would be a total of 1,000 births in 20 years – that being the average life-expectancy. It is the exactness of this archaeologically derived information that is surprising and not the fact for populations in a given socio-economic situation *have* to devise ways of controlling themselves – the alternatives being extinction through decrease on the one hand, or starvation on the other. Though figures vary it is generally accepted that human populations stabilise well below the maximum carrying capacity of the land they inhabit, thus taking account of periodic, unpredictable fluctuations in the available yield to man of the environment. The fineness with which this has to be managed is impressive. As Hassan has calculated, even a growth rate of just 0.1 per cent per annum would theoretically have permitted one original couple to people the world to its present density in 20,000 years. Once a woman becomes pregnant there is a nine-month gestation period which is followed by six months of postpartum sterility – including lactation effects – this giving a maximum possible fertility of a child every 1.25 years. If there were no controlling factors the average woman in an Isbister type community could have had 7.24 children in her breeding life rather than 2.92. The effect of this would have been catastrophic and leads to the question of what exactly the controlling factors were. There are natural ones – though a girl may reach puberty at 15 she generally remains sterile for a year; an estimated 12 per cent of women in a primitive society are in any case sterile; and, similarly, some 12 per cent of pregnancies would have ended in miscarriage or stillbirth. Further, with a maternal mortality of 10–20 per cent a greater number of pregnancies would mean an enhanced risk of dying; this would sharply decrease the life-expectancy of women and, thereby, the average breeding span. Society has its means too, however. As Hassan has noted, marital practices – age of marriage, number of spouses, divorce, widowhood, remarriage and celibacy – and birth control are highly conditioned by social factors which set certain limits on the desired size of the family, the local group, and the child-spacing period. The child-spacing period is particularly important from the woman's point of view. Methods of birth control may have been used – abstinence and coitus interruptus at the least – but primitive societies also widely use means which are, to varying degrees, foreign and even abhorrent to us – abortion and infanticide. In view of the low infant mortality rate given by the human bones found at Isbister I would suggest that the latter practice was used in neolithic Orkney as one means of population control. It is quite reasonable that babies disposed of by this method would not be felt to be part of the community and that their remains would therefore have been excluded from the chamber of the communal tomb. Hassan has pointed out that the natural infant mortality rate in the Neolithic is scarcely likely to have been different from that in the Palaeolithic and that it was probably the lifting of such means of control that permitted the population explosion that went with the discovery of agriculture; subsequent stabilisation of the situation would have involved their reintroduction.

The human bones from Isbister and, to a lesser extent, those from Quanterness have told a lot about the structure of the neolithic population of Orkney and this, in turn, has certain implications for the culture and social structure that existed. The likelihood of infanticide is just one feature of note. High mortality would have posed all sorts of problems in terms of mate selection – or reselection; the care of the young who had lost their natural mother, their natural father, or both; and the accommodation of surviving members of an older generation. Typical societal responses such as the extended family and the lineage come to mind – indeed, the reasons for them become clearer – but it would nevertheless be fascinating to feed the data available into a computer and find out what the problems were and, in particular, what sort of construction residential units might have had. What was the typical neolithic Orcadian 'family' like? It would have been quite different from our own. Then there are the problems concerned with the passing on of knowledge. Some of the information and skills that had to be transmitted to the younger generation were part of the culture shared by everyone – but other aspects were highly specialised, as has been seen in Chapter 4. The average expectation of life at 15 was 9 years for women and 13 for men and some lived beyond that – to be as old as 50 – but there was no way of selecting in advance who of one sex would grow old since death struck indiscriminately. If there were astronomer priests and even administrators in the later Neolithic how were they chosen, and would they each have needed a number of trainees in reserve? The age structure poses even more basic problems. The population was very young – a quarter, in our terms, being pre-school age – and this would necessarily have meant a higher productivity on the part of those members of the society who were of an age to contribute to the economy. One has only to think back to the social reforms of the Victorian era to appreciate that children can work and, again, that it is our present society which is unusual. There would be countless everyday tasks that could have been done by the young and unskilled and, as has already been said, a large proportion of the work involved in the construction of even a chambered tomb could have been carried out by such labour. It is perhaps most significant that one child of six was found to have localised osteoarthritis in the backbone, the most probable cause being the carrying of heavy loads.

What did they look like?

Much of the appearance of human beings is made up of distinctive embellishments – such as hairstyles, clothing and ornaments – and it has to be admitted that current knowledge of these for the Orcadian Neolithic is, at best, slight. Beneath all this, however, is the human being itself and one might still wonder about differences that may have existed. The skeleton is unfortunately an imperfect indicator of the flesh that once surrounded it and has, in any case, changed little in its essential structure for thousands of years. This notwithstanding, the human bones found at Isbister and Quanterness do throw some light upon this fascinating subject.

One old, and firmly rooted, idea which the bones from Isbister absolutely contradict is that people were a great deal smaller in those days than they are now. Chesterman compared the lengths of the long bones for which the sex of the individual could be determined with those of a modern population where the height of the people concerned was known. Since the basic structure of the skeleton has changed little this gave a fairly reliable estimate for the stature of forty-three adult men and women who lived in the Orcadian Neolithic. Men seem on average to have been 5 ft 7 in. tall, and to have ranged from 5 ft 3 in. to 5 ft 10 in.; women similarly averaged 5 ft 3½ in. in height varying from 4 ft 10 in. to 5 ft 4 in. Further, the two heights calculated from bones from Quanterness and the less reliable ones quoted in the reports of earlier excavations confirm this picture. People certainly were slightly shorter than in the present day but the difference is not great and can probably be chiefly attributed to the poor quality of the diet, though genetic factors – race – may have played a part.

A study of the bones from Isbister brought Chesterman to the general conclusion that the group, as a result of environmental conditions, were muscular. He was, moreover, able to determine that this applied to the whole group, the inference being – as would be expected – that there was no leisured class. The legs of the people, in particular, seem to have been well developed, pronounced musculature altering the exact shape of the growing bones. This was a feature that had been noted at Quanterness and at other sites, though the interpretation is novel, but some of the bones from Isbister and Midhowe had the uncommon characteristic of being especially altered at the ankle end. Chesterman's interpretation of this was that hard muscular work must have been undertaken which involved ankles being in a flexed position. One cannot help but wonder why this difference existed between the people at Isbister and, for example, those at Quanterness. My guess is that while no cliffs exist in the neighbourhood of Quanterness, the Isbister territory was fringed with cliffs which could have provided a good annual harvest of eggs and birds. Another feature of special interest is that in a few cases at Isbister, mostly female, there was a markedly increased attachment of the neck muscles to the back of the skull. Chesterman noticed that in such instances there was also a visible depression running across the top of the cranium and his suggestion is that both were caused by carrying loads which were supported by a band over the head. Though such carrying bands are not part of the surviving tradition in Orkney brow bands, at least, are known to have been used in Scotland and in the Faroes. In Orkney it was usual for a load, carried on the back, to be suspended from a rope over the shoulders and, as will be seen, some of the diseased Isbister and Quanterness bones indicate that this method was used in the neolithic period.

None of the other musculature associated with the skull was unusual in any way and it can be assumed that the skin followed the contours of the cranium in an orthodox fashion. This being so, it would theoretically be possible to reconstruct the faces of some of the people at Isbister using forensic tables which give the average depth of soft tissue at various points around the cranium. Such an exercise is sometimes carried out in connection with murder hunts – where the body, when found, has decomposed – and has recently been done very successfully for the skull of Philip II of Macedon. The idea certainly has appeal and is, perhaps, something for the future. For the present measurements of the skull and indices derived from these have to suffice; here, in addition to Chesterman's work there is also that of Elizabeth J. Glenn who independently analysed some of the Isbister crania and compared them with others of both the British Neolithic and Bronze Age. The process she used is too complicated to be described in detail here but it involved the taking of twenty-seven measurements from skulls, the derivation of twelve indices, and the use of a computer programed to throw up the essential differences between samples that were being compared. Her samples were, necessarily, small and this must be borne in mind when evaluating the results.

The first problem to which she addressed herself was the differences between the skulls of the sexes. These had already been sorted on the basis of the types of characteristics described but she was also able to show that women had noticeably smaller heads than men, the difference being quite distinct. This was only to be expected and one might also predict that they would have had different facial features. Two suggestions of this that came out strongly was that the bony housing of the nose in males was marginally longer while females had slightly more elongated eye sockets. It was especially surprising that the males and females seemed to have differently shaped skulls, a feature already brought out by Chesterman's work. An indication of skull type is given by dividing the breadth by the length, those having a cranic index of below 75 being traditionally called 'long headed', or dolichocranic, and those above 75 being similarly termed 'round headed' or mesocranic. Of the thirteen male skulls from Isbister that were sufficiently complete nine were dolichocranic and four mesocranic, while of the six female skulls one was dolichocranic and five mesocranic. Males, in other words, tended to have longer heads than females.

This latter feature would seem to be corroborated by other finds of human bones from contemporary sites on Orkney and I say it is surprising because 'long headed' is usually taken to be indicative of a neolithic population, the supposed incomers of the following period being similarly characterised as being 'round headed'. In consequence of Isbister it now appears that this was not so and the opportunity might be taken here of going a little further into Glenn's comparisons of the skulls with others of neolithic and Bronze Age date. The only additional sample she had for Orkney was from Quanterness but it is nevertheless very interesting that no distinction could be made between the skulls from that site and those from Isbister – the more interesting because the tombs belonged, respectively, to the Grooved Ware and Unstan Ware subcultures. When the skulls of neolithic males from Orkney were compared to those of like date from Arran, however, slight differences could be seen in the facial features and in the ratio of the height of the cranium to its breadth; this distinction was even more marked when the Scottish sample as a whole was contrasted with that from five English sites of the same period. The people in an Isbister type population would not only have been visually distinguishable from those further south in the British Isles but, as a precondition of this, there would have been slight differences in their genes and, therefore, in their precise ancestry. Glenn followed her study through chronologically by contrasting the neolithic male sample as a whole with Bronze Age skulls from the north and west of Scotland. Here she found once again that the major difference lay in changes in facial features and though there was an increase in the height of the head it was confirmed that the shape of the skull given by the cranial index was of less significance than some facial dimensions.

I have spoken of genes and it is worthwhile relating certain peculiarities seen in the human bones from Isbister which may, in varying degrees, have been inherited. The points of articulation of the skull with the vertebra below, the atlas, are known as the occipital condyles, each normally having just one facet. The occurrence of two facets on each side is highly unusual – in one sample of 585 skulls from different countries and periods there were only five instances in 1,144 articulations – yet thirty of the available occipital condyles from Isbister showed this feature – more than a third – and there was even one with treble faceting. A similarly rare occurrence is where the upper facets of the atlas vertebra are divided in the same way and yet out of the forty-five available for inspection at Isbister twenty-two showed this feature – about a half. Again there were eight instances, from six people, of the end bones of thumbs and big toes having an articulation for a third bone which is only present in the other fingers and toes. This in itself is not very unusual, occurring in about 6 per cent of cases, but it may be another genetically transmitted trait. Further unusual occurrences are that there were six examples at Isbister of precocious closure of the sutures of the skull – these being normally estimated at 5 per 10,000 births – and two instances of a horizontal division of the bone below the eyes – Os Japonicum – which is usually found in two or three cases in a thousand. Other interesting occurrences were the incorporation of too many vertebrae in the rigid part of the backbone to which the pelvis attaches – the sacrum – and the fusion of two bones in the toe of a child. The absence of third molars – or wisdom teeth – was more widespread and there was one instance, out of seventy-seven, of a front tooth that was shovel shaped. The latter condition is rare, though at Quanterness three examples were found among the 224 incisors looked at. This catalogue of peculiarities has a particular interest in that some may have been inherited and are therefore indicative of the gene pool peculiar to neolithic Orkney. There is also the possibility – which was tried without success in this instance – that family links in one tomb might be traceable through these and similar characteristics. It is particularly interesting, however, that while the bones of people who were buried at Quanterness showed traits comparable to those from Isbister they were for the most part different, being confined to the first ribs and additional faceting at the junction of the sacrum with the more mobile vertebrae above. Indications such as these may help to discover whether or not groups intermarried; the people of Quanterness and Isbister may have looked similar but the inherited peculiarities of their skeletons were distinct.

Pain, injury and decrepitude

The illnesses of man are of perennial interest and it is only natural to wonder from what bodily woes the neolithic population of Orkney suffered and what was the ultimate cause of their death. There are hints from other sources – the health of women would have been damaged by childbearing and as many as one in three may have died in childbirth – but as the main source of information is the human bones recovered, it is unfortunate that most illnesses – terminal or not – leave little or no trace in the skeleton. One has only to refer to the main causes of death in our own society to appreciate that only a partial view of the situation is possible. The principal cause of death at present, for instance, is disease of the circulatory system – something of which one would hardly expect to obtain surviving evidence. Archaeologists, however, are always hopeful that new information and techniques will permit greater insight; almost unbelievably, Chesterman found indications on vertebrae that one individual at Isbister and another at Quanterness had suffered from hypertension.

It might be considered that a prime cause of injury and death in a primitive society would be the sort of accidental – or non-accidental – physical damage that would result in broken bones. There was certainly no shortage of the latter at either Isbister or Quanterness but few showed any signs of healing or infection; the vast majority therefore had occurred either at the time of death or, most likely, post mortem. The bones had a general tendency to be dry and fragile – this being the result of excarnation – and one can imagine their being unintentionally fractured both by neolithic and subsequent activity in the chambers. The few exceptions – bones that had been broken in the life of the individual – were most interesting. Between Isbister and Quanterness there were four instances of crush injuries to vertebrae, these having been fearfully compressed by an accident such as the individual falling heavily on the base of his or her spine. In the case of an adolescent and an adult man this was not fatal, though the bone disease that set in subsequently would have caused discomfort. Two adults, one female, were, however, less fortunate, the absence of disease implying death within a few months of the mishap. At Isbister there was also evidence for the type of breakages more commonly met with. One man had broken his lower arm, this resulting in an osteoarthritic wrist joint; another had seemingly broken the finer of the two bones in the lower part of one of his legs and though this had healed with little displacement the ligaments remained severely affected; a third adult had broken an ankle bone and, again, osteoarthritis was the cost of recovery. Some ribs from Isbister might also have healed after being broken and this was definitely the case with two from Quanterness. No other breaks, as such, were found among the skeletal material from the latter site but two adults had damaged a knee and a third an elbow to the extent that the bones of the joints became malformed. With the evidence that exists it looks as though something like 2 per cent of individuals suffered a broken bone at some stage in their life and even if this figure is doubled or trebled, to take account of bones that were not put in the chambers, it still makes accidents seem a relatively minor cause of death – the more so since most of the bones broken healed. It also adds to the impression given by a lack of fortifications and weapons that the inhabitants of neolithic Orkney coexisted in comparative peace.

Dental health is a modern concern but even those who take least care are assured of professional help in the case of a crisis. In the neolithic period no such help was at hand. Superficially the teeth found at Isbister and Quanterness seem remarkably healthy, though they did tend to get ground down, presumably as a result of particles of stone from querns having become incorporated in food. Decay was not one of their problems – only nine out of 1,537 teeth available showed the cavities we associate with toothache and in this respect, if in few others, their diet was better than ours. However, once infection of any sort had set in it had to run its course. At both Isbister and Quanterness there were indications of periodontal disease and at the former site five instances of abscesses in the sockets of molars. These must have been extremely painful and one can feel for a man aged 45–50 who had an abscess which took in the area of all three back teeth on one side of the upper jaw. There were also tumours. A thirty-five-year-old woman – the one whose bones were lifted separately – had a cyst in the upper palate which left a depression in the bone measuring 28 by 18 by 18 mm! This appears to have arisen from one of the canine teeth and, though shown by X-ray analysis to be benign, it must have been unpleasant in the extreme. Similarly, an adolescent male from the same site had a cyst in his lower jaw; though benign this had turned septic and one of the molar teeth had apparently been ejected. Damage to teeth could not be remedied. At Quanterness there was one incisor which had been split to the root and, very peculiarly, the root of a molar had seemingly been cut in antiquity by a sharp instrument. Malpositioned teeth, too, had to stay as they were – there were no braces. This is cosmetic and will raise little sympathy in the reader – but what of impacted teeth? Six wisdom teeth and three canines were affected in this way at Isbister and the unrelievable pain they must have caused some of their possessors would have been excruciating. .

Three men and two women at Isbister also suffered from something which is technically known as temporo-mandibular joint dysfunction. This means that the lower jaw did not articulate properly and its movements would have caused recurrent dislocation – though of a temporary and minor nature. Typically this would have resulted in crepitation and clicking sounds when eating or speaking which would have been accompanied by muscular spasms and discomfort. An even more serious condition than this – one that may have been terminal – was apparent in a rather small skull from the same site which belonged to an old man of 45–50 years of age. This was sufficiently broken at the front to show that the upper part of the skull was of abnormal thickness – 14 mm! X-ray analysis disproved a provisional diagnosis of Paget's disease and demonstrated hypoplasia of the diploë – the cancellous tissue between the inner and outer surfaces. Though the thickness of the diploë does vary, such an extreme case must have been pathological and it appears to have produced asymmetry in the foramen magnum. The latter is the hole at the base of the cranium through which the spinal cord passes and the condition is liable to have been a very serious one.

The above cases all apply to a few individuals but what is most telling about the health of neolithic people in Orkney as a whole is the prevalence of degenerative diseases such as osteoarthritis, osteophytosis, intervertebral disc lesions and osteochondritis dissecans. Degenerative disease of the spine in adults at once stands out as a common condition. At Isbister, for example, some of the vertebrae were found from the bodies of seventy adults and it would appear even from this partial evidence that thirty-three had suffered from degenerative spinal disease. This gives an incidence of 47 per cent and there can be no doubt that the true occurrence was higher still. It is particularly staggering when one considers the average age of death for adults of each sex. Nor did the young escape entirely, for evidence of osteoarthritis was found in the neck vertebrae of both a child of six years and a youth aged 13–14. The picture given by the human bones from Quanterness is similar – except that a third of the cases of spinal disease there were diagnosed from the bones of individuals who did not survive their adolescence.

Perhaps significantly, osteoarthritis was not as common in other parts of the body as it was in the back. Curiously, at least eight of the people buried at Isbister had it in their big toe and this peculiar condition may have been even more prevalent for the bones concerned were found only rarely. It is possible, as with the enhanced musculature of the ankles, that this is a reflection of the exact nature of the environment in which they lived. Thirteen rib fragments from Isbister also showed osteo-arthritis and, though this condition is not unknown in Western Europe, eight instances of it were found at Quanterness and it has also been found among human bones of neolithic date from sites excavated in England. Chesterman has linked this with the localised osteoarthritis also seen in some neck vertebrae and considers both to have been the result of carrying loads by a strap or rope running across the neck and under the opposite armpit. The explanation offered is particularly attractive since this was a widely adopted means of carrying burdens in Orkney up to comparatively recent times.

The approach taken has necessarily been on the basis of individual bones rather than dwelling on the multiple ills of particular people. This is an unavoidable result of the practice of excarnated partial burial and the manner in which the site was excavated. Had the bodies of the dead been deposited entire in the chamber things would have been different and even though this was not the case our knowledge of particular individuals would certainly have been enhanced by painstaking recovery and recording; it is to be hoped that some future site, as undisturbed as Isbister, will render such an excavation possible. As it is there is just one person who was buried at Isbister who can be considered as an individual – her bones formed the excarnated burial that was lifted separately from the floor of the chamber. Though only a proportion of her skeleton was represented this was sufficient to throw light on at least a few aspects of her existence. She was small, even for a woman, being only 4 ft 10¾ in. high and, probably through inheritance, she had a double facet on the vertebra below her skull – though this would not have caused any inconvenience. Work under-taken during her youth had increased the muscularity of her upper legs to the extent that the exact shape of the bones was altered and two of her ribs had the localised osteoarthritis which can probably be associated with the carrying of burdens. She suffered from a degenerative disease in the bones of the upper part of her back and had a massive, and very unpleasant, cyst in the roof of her mouth. She died at the age of around thirty-five, a comparatively old woman.

6 · Daily Life

Farmer, hunter, fisherman, gatherer

When neolithic man first came to Orkney, around 4,000–3,500 BC, it was virgin territory. There was no earlier population to contend with and he was free to settle the land and exploit it in the fully developed ways he brought with him. In a way Orkney can be seen as a neolithic New World, a land unfettered by the past which could be moulded according to the established practices of neolithic times. Archaeologists are uncertain where the immigrants came from; nowadays, theories about the movement of 'cultures' are not propounded with the confidence of earlier decades. However, it seems probable that the Unstan Ware element arrived via the north of Scotland – there being firm, and earlier, links across the Pentland Firth – while the route of those belonging to the Grooved Ware subculture may – and I only say may – have been via the West Coast. It is not implied that the full complement of population came at once for no doubt it was a gradual, though short-term, process in which there was a certain manoeuvring for position and where immigration was replaced in time by internal population growth. Perhaps the situation can be pictured as an initial phase of settlement followed by one of consolidation in which the whole land was peopled by groups which splintered off when populations grew beyond that suitable for single territories. Here there was an element of change and, in any case, neolithic society, once formed, should not be thought of as being static. Societies change over the years, however slowly, and, in the case of Orkney, a transition has been noted which culminated in a centralised social organisation. Behind all this, however, there were basic needs which a society of any type has to meet.

Arguably the foremost of these would have been the necessity to obtain food and the manner in which this was done is taken as a first theme.

The first settlers were farmers – this is the basis of the Neolithic Revolution and all that came from it – and in such a society the bulk of the food, the largest percentage of the calorific intake, would have been from crops. This gives an opportunity to underline the preparations necessary for successful immigration. Not only would the incomers have had to bring with them sufficient seed to plant their first crop but they would also have needed enough grain to feed them until they harvested that crop. This suggests strongly that they were an overspill from settled groups with a flourishing and soundly based economy and the likelihood is that they did not come from very far away. Analysis of pollen from the neighbourhood of Isbister indicates that fields were made by clearing scrub tree cover – almost certainly with the aid of mounted, polished stone axe-heads. From preference sandy soils would have been chosen – such as those around Skara Brae, the Knap of Howar, and the Links of Noltland – since these were easiest to work with primitive implements, and the heavier gleys of the valley bottoms would have been avoided. Parallel lines gouged in the sub-soil, as found at the Links of Noltland, indicate that fields were worked with a simple form of plough called an ard. Hundreds of the pecked and shaped sandstone working points of these are known from the Northern Isles, though the only one found in a neolithic context so far is that from Isbister itself. Practical experiment has shown that the land would have had to be broken before an ard was used since, otherwise, whether the traction was human or animal, the ard point would not have penetrated. This would have been the case particularly with land which had been left fallow for a while or which had been freshly cleared. Implements which may have been used to break the land are the ox shoulder blades, as found at Skara Brae and the Links of Noltland, and the stone mattock heads, as found at Isbister itself. These would also have served to produce a final tilth. Though only small areas have been examined the excavations at the Links of Noltland have shown that fields were, on occasion, bounded by walls or by ditches. There is evidence from Skara Brae and the Knap of Howar for cereal in the form of carbonised seeds and pollen grains and in impressions found on pots, especially those from Unstan tomb. It is the charred remains of processed grain from the floor of Isbister, however, which give us the most information for here there was barley and, to a lesser extent, wheat, both being mixed with the seeds of weeds which grew with them. Microscopic analysis of the flints from the Links of Noltland should reveal whether any had been set in sickles but the crop could have been harvested by hand before threshing.

If no action was taken then the fertility of the fields would soon have been depleted. The initial response may simply have been to clear new areas, leaving previous ones fallow, but the pressure of an increasing population on a finite amount of arable land would have made manuring desirable. There is evidence from the Links of Noltland both that animal manure was used and that settlement midden was weathered and then spread on areas which were under cultivation. The artificial building up of such rich soil is well attested for other periods in Orkney. Part of the process may have involved taking seaweed from the beach – this being the most likely explanation for the presence of tiny marine shells found at the Knap of Howar. Even with manuring the situation was, ultimately, an unstable one. Scrub trees that were cleared could not re-establish themselves because of the feeding of animals and the land, in general, became bare, worked out and acidic. With a climatic deterioration involving lower temperatures and increased rainfall, blanket peat formed and this more than offset the technological innovations of the period following the Neolithic – the Bronze Age.

The Pentland Firth is rough and wide and though it is conceivable that deer might have swum across, in general it remains true to say that the animals of neolithic Orkney were there because man had brought them. This indicates that the

first settlement was not haphazard or chance. The best information at present available on the types of animals involved comes
from bones found at the Knap of Howar, which have been
analysed by Barbara Noddle. It would seem that the cattle were
large, the lightest of them overlapping the heaviest weights
found for later animals. They were almost as heavy as wild cattle
– aurox – and so Noddle thinks that they were comparatively
recent domesticates. The sheep, similarly, were smaller than
their wild counterparts and they were not very far removed
from the primitive breed currently found in North Ronaldsay
where the islanders follow an old tradition of walling them off
from the cultivated land and allowing them to live mainly on
seaweed. It must be said at this point that sheep and goat bones
are notoriously difficult to distinguish and that both species
were probably present. The measurement of the pig bones also
indicates large animals, overlapping with the dimensions of the
present-day wild sow. There is no secure evidence for horses in
neolithic Orkney but there were dogs and, doubtless, these
were useful in handling herds of sheep, goats, and cattle.

The evidence from all the settlement sites points to sheep/
goats and cattle having been kept in approximately equal proportions. Pigs by comparison were rare, being kept and fattened
only in small numbers. No structures which might have housed
animals have been found to date and it is most likely that they
were left simply to graze, the climate being slightly warmer
then. There are indications from Shetland that land used for
this purpose was fired periodically in autumn in order to burn
off the old grass and its competing species so that fresh shoots
were available. There is also an increasing amount of evidence
for stock management with animals generally being killed
young, only a small number being kept for breeding. The old
explanation of this was 'autumnal killing' – the idea being
that stock could not have been overwintered in great numbers
because of a shortage of feed. This is no doubt true but there
may have been other reasons. Calves and lambs may have been
killed at or soon after birth because their mothers' milk was

desired for human consumption. Similarly, young animals may have been slaughtered because their meat was preferred and perhaps because their skins were thinner and more flexible. Whatever the case it can be seen that the age of animals sacrificed at Isbister fits with the knowledge which the settlements have given of the stock policy of the times.

The hunting of animals must have been restricted to deer and even these may have been herded and managed – though the amount of venison consumed was minimal compared to mutton, goat flesh or beef – the latter being the most common by virtue of the carcass size of the animal. This notwithstanding, the discovery at the Links of Noltland of a cluster of some thirteen articulated deer skeletons, mostly from young animals, is of interest as it may indicate culling and is certainly evidence for a tremendous waste of resources (Fig. 38). Such 'waste' is often associated with ritual and the mass of deer antlers in the small tomb at the north end of the tiny Holm of Papa Westray should not be forgotten. The Links of Noltland also provides us with a deer butchery site, the bones remaining being those of the head and extremities.

The commonest quarry of the hunter was surely birds, which, though of scarcely any significance as a proportion of the food intake, would have added variety and fat to the diet. It must not be forgotten, too, that certain sea birds may have been hunted for the oil in their flesh – this being boiled off and used for culinary, lighting, and, perhaps, medicinal purposes. The plumage of some birds may have been what was desired and we must not forget that sea eagles were caught at Isbister for ritual rather than practical reasons. The list of species represented at the Knap of Howar alone is a very long one. As would be expected they are predominantly birds which take their food from the open sea, mainly in the form of fish, small crustaceans, and other marine organisms; the best represented of these was the great auk, a now extinct, large, flightless creature. Such birds could most easily be taken when nesting on land and in the cliffs – as was the case until recently on the island of St Kilda,

Fig. 38   Deer skeletons found in the recent excavations at the Links of Noltland

where they played a vital part in the economy. It is interesting that the skulls and foot bones of the great auks were absent at the Knap of Howar, suggesting that the birds were butchered at the shore by removing the heads and feet and probably the viscera to make the carcass more portable. There can be little doubt that eggs, too, were gathered and indeed shells have been found at Skara Brae and the Links of Noltland. Other birds would not have been so easily caught. Don Bramwell has even suggested that boats might have been used to secure divers. Bird species that inhabit the land are usually wary and none more so than geese, ducks and swans. Hunting them involves careful stalking and the use of projectiles such as arrows. It would by no means have been easy. In the context of this book possible methods of catching sea eagles are of particular interest. They could have been taken from the cliffs during the breeding season and, indeed, 'as nimble as an Orkney eagle-catcher' was a phrase current in the nineteenth century – the extinction of the birds bearing testimony to this peculiar skill. Usually, eagles are disliked by farmers, who feel them to be in competition, and an alternative method of capture used recently in Scandinavia is to render them flightless. This can be done by either putting bait in a narrow trench or by letting the birds gorge themselves on a laid-out carcass.

It will be remembered that the fish from Isbister were almost entirely small ones and species which could have been taken in shallow water. On their own they give evidence for the possible use of baited nets, spears, and rods and line – though some could have been left in pools by the receding tide. Among the bones found at the Knap of Howar were those from large species, e.g., cod and ling weighing 10 kg, a turbot of 5 kg, a flounder of 2 kg, conger eels as long as 1.5 m, and a halibut which would have weighed as much as 40 kg. This is evidence not only for offshore fishing in deep waters but also for hooks or gorges and lines as much as 40 m long which could take the considerable strain involved. Fishing, clearly, was an important source of food, though how important has yet to be determined.

The most probable bait used was shellfish and this may be taken to account for a proportion of the tens of thousands of shells found on habitation sites – something like 80,000 have been recovered from just the small area investigated to date at the Links of Noltland. Some may also have been used for human consumption; though limpets predominate there are other shellfish which are more palatable and of less use for fishing. At the Knap of Howar, for example, 7 per cent of the sea shells were from oysters, 2 per cent winkles, 1 per cent cockles, and 0.5 per cent razor shells. Oysters, winkles and cockles are known, if not universally appreciated, delicacies and could have been obtained, respectively, by diving, picking off rocks, and raking the sand below high water mark. Many a visitor to Orkney will have been puzzled by people walking slowly backwards close to the sea along the beach at an ebb tide. They are looking for 'spoots', the name given locally to razor shells since any pressure makes them send up a jet of water as they burrow down and, their presence having been betrayed, they can be jammed in their burrows with a knife or garden fork and then dug out. Even limpets were a source of sustenance in hard times in Orkney as late as the nineteenth century and may therefore have formed part of the diet in the New Stone Age. Nevertheless it is astonishing that for all the number of shells found shellfish, as a whole, could not have made a major contribution to life in terms of the number of calories they provide. Even the most favourable of the figures available suggest that 10,000 limpets would provide sufficient calories to support only four family groups – some twenty-four people – for one day.

It can be seen that the quest for food meant exploitation of resources to the full. The seeds of weeds may have been collected – for there is evidence of their being processed – and fruits and nuts, particularly those of the hazel, may have been used, as may fungi. Similarly, it is known from Isbister and the Links of Noltland that edible crabs were caught and, this being the case, there is no reason why the occasional lobster should not have been taken too. There is also evidence from several of the sites that whales and seals were butchered; the whales would have been stranded on the beach either accidentally or after a flotilla of boats had driven them into the shallows. Information from the Knap of Howar shows that the seals killed there were diseased and perhaps the most easily caught of the herd.

Such variety and seeming abundance would, however, have been seasonal and there can be little doubt that neolithic man came to grips with the problem of preserving foodstuffs for winter use. In Shetland nowadays mutton is pickled and dried and sausages smoked; in Orkney it is common to see salted split fish left out on fine days; and on St Kilda there was the habit of splitting young sea birds down the back and preserving them. Similarly, eggs will keep in ash, grain stays good unless it moulders, and most vegetable stuffs can be dried with varying success. Such preservation would have been vital to the economy though, as yet, the means employed by neolithic man can only be guessed at.

Craftsmanship and housekeeping

Ethnographic parallels make it clear that it would be unwise to project modern notions of gender roles too rigidly into the past. It is likely that women kept house just as it is probable that men were concerned with outdoor activities such as hunting and fishing, but when it comes to such matters as making pots or clothes, or wearing ornaments and even cosmetics, then it is simply not known what the situation was. That there were sexually defined roles is almost certain but the exact lines of demarcation are beyond our present knowledge.

The neolithic people of Orkney used the resources of their environment for craft purposes with the same facility shown in their exploitation of it for basic foodstuffs. One little detail is sufficient to show this. Clay for pottery was widely available but as is almost always the case with this material there was a need to add tempering in order to give it body, reduce its plasticity in manufacture, and make it fire better. As elsewhere crushed shell, old vessels, and stone were often used for this purpose but David Williams of Southampton University has discovered a 'technological recipe' of particular interest through examining thin sections of pottery with the aid of a geological microscope. It would seem that the Grooved Ware people, in particular, often added crushed rock taken from volcanic extrusions, dykes, and would think nothing of going two miles to collect this special material. This has thermal characteristics which are similar to clay and the clearly intended result was pots which would not break either when fired or when used for cooking – a form of prehistoric Pyrex. The clay having been prepared it was rolled into lengths and formed into pots, each successive coil being moulded into that below. The Unstan Ware people had the subcultural trait of making round-based vessels, of which some were deep and others bowl-shaped with a distinctive collar around the rim (Pl. 19; Fig. 26); the Grooved Ware people, on the other hand, held to their tradition of pots which were bucket shaped and which had flat bases (Fig. 39). In either case the vessel shape was probably perfected by hitting the pot with a flat implement while an otherwise static former was moved around its interior. In some cases pots were then decorated. The Unstan Ware people largely confined this to their characteristic bowls and it was probably bone points which were used to puncture and slash the clay around the outside of the collars; some of the decoration, particularly at Isbister, was made with the potter's fingernails. The Grooved Ware people also applied cordons and blobs of clay, sometimes pinching these to enhance the effect. The result of the process so far was pots which were perfectly shaped but which had a rough surface resulting from the tempering in the clay. They were therefore dipped into a suspension of clay in water in order that this should be masked by a slip. After being dried until 'leather hard' Unstan Ware pottery was then often burnished – presumably with a bone implement – this not only making the surface shiny but also making the vessel less permeable to liquid. Having been dried out

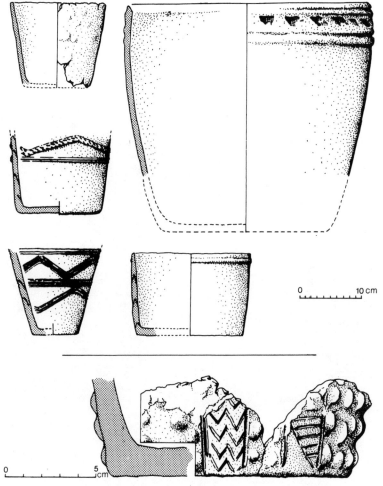

Fig. 39 Grooved Ware from Skara Brae, Stenness and Quanterness

thoroughly pots were then fired, and for this nothing more sophisticated than a bonfire would have been necessary.

The subject of implements has been raised and should perhaps be pursued at a general level. Bone was one invaluable source and indeed when Anna Ritchie found the bulk of the skeletal remains in the midden at the Knap of Howar to be

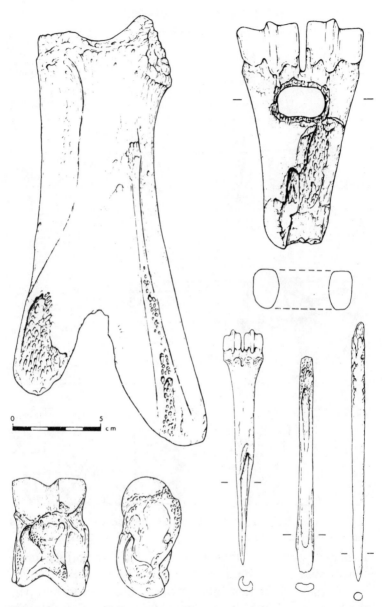

Fig. 40   Bone artefacts from the Links of Noltland. From top left:
scapula shovel; metapodial ?adze; astragalus polisher; metapodial
point; spatulate implement; pin

fragmentary she concluded that this was because they had been worked over as a raw material – though an alternative explanation is that they were broken to extract marrow. This situation is in distinct contrast to that found in the tombs. Particular bones were favoured for the manufacture of different tool types, in accordance with the suitability of their natural shape. At Skara Brae, for instance, gannet humeri were shaped to make piercers while there and elsewhere the broad flat blades of cattle scapulae were used as hand shovels. Among the bones more commonly utilised were metapodials from the feet of sheep or goats, the shaft of these being sliced off obliquely and fashioned to either a point or a broad gouge shape (Fig. 40). In this and in the manufacture of similar tools pumice, picked off the beach, would have been of service. The much larger metapodials of cattle were sometimes treated similarly, and a hole bored through them so that they could be mounted, and perhaps used as adzes. Ankle bones of animals – astragali – were used as polishers, perhaps leather burnishers – while slivers of bone were turned to all sorts of uses. Some were made into needles, others are spatulate, and one from the Knap of Howar may be either a gorge – used in place of a hook when fishing – or part of a barbed fish spear.

Stone was also a useful raw material from which tools could be created and the most useful of all was flint or chert, the hardness and sharpness of which would have done much to make up for the lack of knowledge about metals. Flint and chert cannot be mined in Orkney but nodules do occur in the glacial clay and they are also found on certain beaches. The nodules gathered were flaked using hammers such as stone or antler. Sometimes an anvil was used to support the nodule and assist flaking from the core (Fig. 41). The flakes removed would have been very sharp and quite serviceable as they stood, but they could also be shaped and altered by retouching. This process may be carried out by pressure flaking along the edges of a flake using a blunt instrument, such as a piece of bone or an antler tine, or coarser retouch may be achieved with a percussor, often

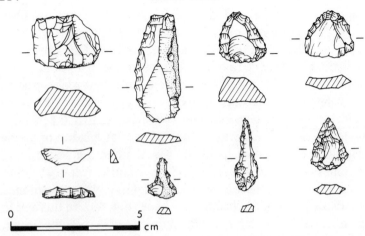

Fig. 41 Flint objects from the Links of Noltland. From top left:
core; edge retouched flake; 2 scrapers; scraper resharpening flake; 2
Grobust picks; leaf-shaped point or arrowhead

of stone. In some cases, flakes may have been subjected to a
carefully controlled heat treatment to make them easier to
retouch. Leaf-shaped arrowheads were one desired object and
these would obviously have required much alteration of the
original flake blanks, and that towards a fairly clear purpose,
but scrapers and fine edge retouched pieces, blades, were
amongst the variety of other tools produced, many of which
needed less work. A particular type of implement which has
recently been recognised in work by Caroline Wickham-Jones,
following the Links of Noltland excavations, is the tiny 'Grobust
pick' which was possibly used as a piercer or drill bit. The
sandstone, so common in Orkney, was also used in a variety of
ways even, on occasion, being retouched. As has been seen ard
points and mattocks were manufactured but there were also
querns and a crude but efficient edged implement known as a
Skaill knife was made by the simple process of smashing beach
boulders. Polished stone must also be taken account of here.
Most commonly axe-heads and mace-heads were made from
specially selected hard stones, the latter also being fashioned

from antler. Knives are also known, such as the unfinished one from Isbister. Manufacturing polished stone implements would have been a laborious process with a chipped rough-out being ground – probably on a coarse stone and using sand – until the object was ready for its final polishing. The perforations of mace-heads, in particular, are testimony to a high level of expertise and they may have been produced by grinding, suitably worn pointed stones having been found. However, the use of the drill was known as well.

Brief mention should also be given to the type of implements and artefacts of which there is, as yet, little or no knowledge. Part of the recent excavations at Skara Brae was devoted to a waterlogged layer with conditions suitable for the preservation of organic objects which would otherwise have rotted away. Two finds – a wooden handle and some rope of twisted heather – provide an idea of what is generally missing on other sites and it is possible to imagine all sorts of wooden articles and perhaps baskets similar to those made to this day in Orkney from straw and other vegetation. Skins should also not be forgotten for, at the least, they may have served as water containers.

It will be apparent that to associate any of these known implements with particular processes of manufacture is likely to be merely a matter of conjecture, no matter how probable it may seem. This will not always be the case, however, for work is currently being undertaken on artefacts from the Links of Noltland which should transform our approach and increase our understanding. The fact is that even implements of as hard a material as flint are affected by the things they are used on. Such wear patterns, usually invisible to the naked eye, can be studied under the microscope and compared to test patterns produced by using a similar implement on a range of likely materials. The results of this can be very impressive indeed. Some quartz implements from Shetland have recently been analysed in this manner by Rosemary Bradley and it has been ascertained that some were used in a certain direction for cutting meat while others were used to scrape hides.

There is no definite evidence that neolithic people in Orkney knew how to either spin or weave and the probability is that clothes and coverings were fashioned from skins. As has been noted, this may be one reason why animals were killed young, the skins of calves and lambs being thinner and more supple. The hide could have been cut from the carcass with a flint knife and then stretched out for curing on a wooden frame with bone pins possibly having been used to position and tension it. Flint scrapers and even pumice could have been employed to take off adherent fat and rubbed-in salt might have been used to prevent decay, the cured stiff skin being made supple again with oil taken from seabirds, seals or whales. Skins thus prepared could have been cut to shape with flint knives and sewn together with a needle and thong passed through holes made by a bone piercer. Unlike the pottery, where the finished article is commonly found, this process can be seen only as a chain of supposition but there is hope that one day neolithic garments will be recovered – examples of such date being known from further afield – and the microscopic analysis of implements should tell us much.

Given the space available a review such as this must be even more patchy than our knowledge of the subject. The processing of food and its cooking is, for example, a wide area to which only scant reference can be made. After the animals had been killed – and one young bull at Skara Brae seemed definitely to have been pole-axed – they would have been eviscerated, skinned, the extremities chopped off and discarded, and the dressed carcass jointed. The slaughtering of stock would not have been a frequent occurrence and judging from comparatively recent practices among the rural population of Orkney meat would have been shared out and much of it pickled, such fare only really being eaten on festive and other special occasions. Grain, taken from store, could have been broken by pounding it in a mortar or ground into flour beneath a rubbing stone pushed backwards and forwards along a saddle quern. Certain of the rubbing stones from the Knap of Howar were of particular interest since they had a pecked hollow in their worked surface and ethnographic parallels suggest they may have been used for grinding wild seeds, this peculiar feature catching the seeds up in order that they be crushed the more effectively. Such foodstuffs may have ended up as gruel or stews – some species of boiled sustenance – no doubt supplemented by wild turnips and other edible roots, fruits and leaves of plants. Pots are frequently burnt on the outside from having been placed in embers and some – such as a few from Isbister – have knobs or holes by which they could have been suspended. There were, however, other methods of cooking available. Meat could obviously have been roasted – this being suitable for large joints – and a variety of victuals from gulls' eggs to unleavened bread can be cooked on a stone slab laid on a glowing fire. There were also ovens, one being known from Rinyo and another possible one from the Links of Noltland. It is not to be supposed that food would necessarily have been very basic. Given eggs, cheese, butter, milk, yoghurt, honey, flour, fat, nuts, oil, meat, fish, game, seafood and a whole range of vegetable products a great variety of dishes *could* have been prepared.

The main source of fuel up until recently in Orkney was peat but this was, in general, unavailable to neolithic man, being a product of his denudation of the land and the climatic deterioration of the Bronze Age. Among the alternative sources of heat are a few that might be surprising – such as dried dung, turf, dry seaweed, and the bones of whales and seals. Sanday and North Ronaldsay are both without peat and up until the first decades of this century 'coo's scones' were a favourite, the material being gathered from the grass, cut from a winter midden – when it contained straw – and moulded by hand. Sometimes it was mixed with turfy earth to form a kind of peat. One nineteenth-century observer commented that it 'emitted an unsavoury reek that tickles the inexperienced nostril. The islanders eat with relish fish that have been smoked with these dried dung cakes.' If thoroughly dried it will burn with a clear flame and with no more smell than wood. Seaweed was collected, too, the fuel for one winter being gathered the year before and dried in the intervening summer. The problem with this was that it burned fast and was more suited to cooking than giving long-term heat. The effect of all this effort was, in reality, to provide little fuel and as Alexander Fenton has recorded and commented mothers might have had to lie in bed the whole day with their infants to keep them warm, while hypothermia may have been a common cause of death in older people. The search for fuel also denuded the natural environment, land being skimmed for turf and manure being burnt rather than put back into the cycle of nature and one can project this back into neolithic times when additional damage was doubtless done by the cutting of such thickets as remained after agriculture and domestic animals had taken their toll. There was, however, a source of fuel – and building material – which is less apparent today than it would have been then. Driftwood is avidly collected on the beaches today, but in neolithic times the volume of this would have been swollen by fallen timber from virgin forests as far distant as the Americas. It is impossible to say how great the supply would have been but spruce has been identified at Skara Brae – as it has at a number of other early coastal Scottish sites – and the roofing of one neolithic building in Shetland is calculated to have involved some 700 m of dressed timber.

It would be misleading to give the impression that neolithic man in Orkney laboured the whole while. The islands would have supported a neolithic economy of comparative richness and people would have had more leisure than if, for example, they had been peasants under the oppressive demands of feudal overlords. The building of tombs and circle-henges imply that life was not a hand-to-mouth existence but that there was time to spare for other activities. Some of these would have been ceremonial and communal but there would have been other more personal ways of passing the time about which little is known. It is certain, however, that they had the leisure to ornament their persons for beads have been found in huge numbers, particularly at Skara Brae and the Links of Noltland.

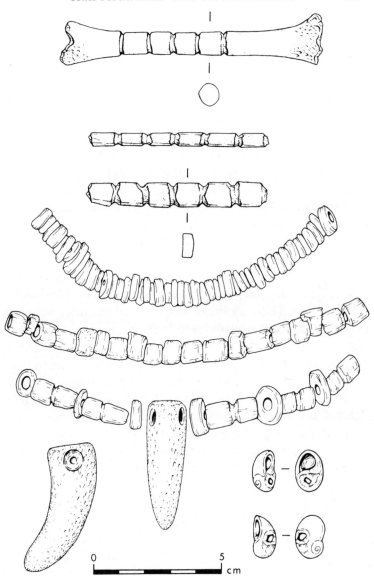

Fig. 42   Beads and their manufacture as illustrated by finds from Skara Brae and the Links of Noltland

Those similar to the Isbister ones were manufactured by cutting roundels from lengths of bone, teeth, shells or antler, drilling a perforation as necessary and rubbing them smooth (Fig. 42); sometimes they were artificially coloured. According to Andrew Foxon, who is studying the bone artefacts from the Links of Noltland, the labour involved in producing a string of such polished beads would have been prodigious. There are certainly several ethnographic parallels for such things being a medium of exchange – a primitive form of currency – or forming gifts intended to reinforce social links and produce indebtedness. It must be borne in mind that 2,400 beads of this type were in a cache in the side cell of one of the Skara Brae houses. Other beads were made more simply by rubbing winkles on a stone until a second hole was produced. When taken from an archaeological context – bleached, brittle, and often broken – such beads are unimpressive but fresh brown and yellow striped shells, graded for size, and threaded together make very beautiful necklaces. There are other types of bead and there were also pendants, some of pigs' tusks, others of carved ivory, and the dog's tooth in the infill at Isbister must not be forgotten. These, however, are only the surviving traces of personal ornamentation in dress and much could have been done with feathers, dyed leather and the like. Childe found stone palettes at Skara Brae still bearing traces of red ochre and the same material has been found in limpet shells during the more recent excavations. It is quite possible that this – and other material, such as lamp-black – were used to pattern the body and face.

Some idea of the art of the times can be gained from the decorations that exist on pots and on a few other types of artefact. There are also carvings on stone, the best known of these being at Skara Brae and on the walls of the long Maes Howe type tomb at the south end of the Holm of Papa Westray. All is geometric, and nothing naturalistic. The heights that could be achieved in this style are exemplified by a quite recent discovery – a large carved stone found in two parts on the lip of a quarry at Pierowall in Westray (Fig. 43). Almost certainly this

Fig. 43 Megalithic art on a stone found recently on the rim of Pierowall Quarry on Westray

work of art was originally associated with the chambered tomb which Niall Sharples investigated there as part of a consequent archaeological salvage operation. The piece is impressive in the simplicity of its design and the skill of its execution, though what meaning the symbols may have had – if any – at present remains a mystery.

It will have been noted that the economy of neolithic Orkney was quite self-sufficient. It is known, however, that there was contact with other groups since there are parallels in the spheres of both material culture and social organisation. There was in the late Neolithic, after all, a concept of measurement, geometry, and astronomy which was uniform over Britain, and beyond. In a tribal world such contact almost certainly implies exchange and indeed an exchange network of pottery vessels – and perhaps their contents – and of stone axes is well documented for other parts of the country. One axe found in Orkney is made of porcellanite from Tievebulliagh or Brockley in County Antrim; another is seemingly of riebeckite felsite from Shetland.

The habitations of the living

It is no wonder that a century elapsed between the initial discovery of Skara Brae and the realisation of its true age. It still remains almost incredible that a domestic site belonging to so remote a period as the Stone Age should be found in such a perfect state. The sand which engulfed Skara Brae was, in its way, as miraculous an agent of preservation as the lava which overwhelmed Pompeii, the permafrost that deep-froze the Scythian tombs, and the aridity that arrested decay in the pyramids of Ancient Egypt. Appreciation of the antiquity of the site came when the pottery from it and Rinyo was fitted in the evolving sequence for prehistoric Britain as a whole but now, as a consequence of David Clarke's excavation, we have a good series of radiocarbon dates as well. In common with other similar determinations these have pushed back the time scale and have additionally shown that Skara Brae was occupied for a long period – from about 3100 BC to 2450 BC – some 650 years. The houses are not just remarkable for their preservation, age and duration, but for the degree of planning involved and the skill, even sophistication, with which it was executed. One's estimation of the capabilities possessed by the neolithic population of Orkney is raised by every visit.

What one sees is largely the uppermost structures – the earlier ones being still concealed beneath them. The remains are self-evidently those of a village (Fig. 44), as many as six conjoined houses being connected by passageways and the whole being served by a common drainage system. The houses are solidly built with walls which are up to 3 m thick and which, in places, remain preserved to a standing height exceeding 2.5 m. When speaking of their 'standing height', however, one is considering the structures only from their interior for they were recessed into earlier midden; this material was also used to pack the centre of the walls, and further refuse was banked around them when built. The effect was to make the village largely subterranean, this device having been used up to the recent past in Orkney in order to combat the chilling effects of the wind. The passages are lintelled over but one of the questions most commonly asked of the custodian is how the houses were roofed, the largest being just over 6 m square. When the site was excavated by Childe the only answer that seemed likely was that the ribs of whales were used to provide a superstructure but there is now a greater awareness of the volume and type of driftwood that would have been available and there is no reason why this, the most obvious material, should not have been used. It is true that the internal furnishings of the houses are fashioned from stone – such as survive – but as David Clarke has observed, this may have been purely a matter of preference. One can still see the remains of nineteenth-century buildings in Orkney where a framework of driftwood rafters was placed on the wallhead, augmented with simmons – ropes of twisted

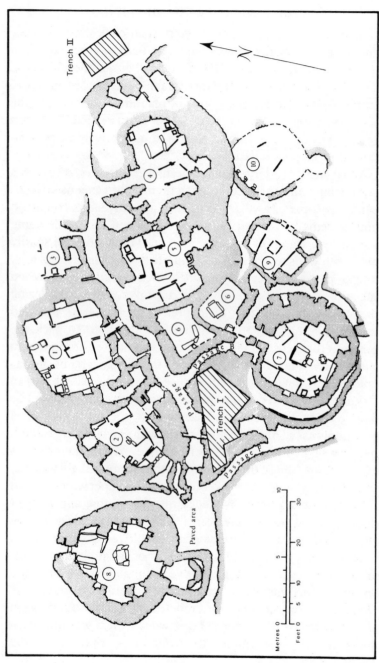

Fig. 44   The neolithic village of Skara Brae. The location of the trenches of the recent excavations are shown

vegetation as found at Skara Brae – this pitched base then being covered with overlapping turves. There may have been a smoke-hole in the roof, though – judging from some pre-1800 houses in both the Northern and Western Isles – there would have been no necessity for this, as the smoke could curl out under the eaves. There may also have been skylights, perhaps filled with a frame over which a bladder or an untanned, defleeced lambskin was stretched. It is impossible to be certain.

The houses to be seen at Skara Brae are all very similar in plan, except one which is separate and to the west, and which may have been a workshop. There are differences, most notably that the beds of the earliest buildings are recessed into the walls rather than projecting from them, but the overall impression is one of great uniformity and continuity. This being the case it will be sufficient to visit just one of the houses – No 1 (Pl. 22). There may have originally been more than one entrance to the complex, perhaps three, but that which survives is to the west where, to the outside, there is an area of paving. Passing over the latter one would have had to crouch to enter the passage – this having been a factor in the erroneous belief that neolithic people were a great deal smaller in stature than present-day man. Two doors had then to be negotiated, the sills, jambs and bolt holes for these still being clearly visible. It is doubtful if these doors were in any way defensive, and they may have functioned to baffle the wind, but they add to the impression given of a closely knit community whose members cooperated in the planning of their village and the provision of common facilities. The lintels of the passage were closely placed and almost certainly covered over by midden. One would therefore have had to feel one's way in the dark, passing the door to house 2 on the left, the passage leading to house 7 on the right, and then coming round a narrow bend before reaching the entrance to house 1. If someone was inside then the door may well have been in place – this being perhaps made of wood or just a stone slab; in eighteenth-century Orkney a straw mat sometimes sufficed. This would have given privacy and stopped off draughts but was hardly intended to be a protection from pilfering neighbours since it could be bolted only from the inside. Whether or not smoke-holes or skylights existed, the interior of the house entered would have been very dark, the major source of light probably being a fire smouldering within the central, square, kerbed hearth. Perhaps the most lasting impression on a time-traveller would be the smell – a mingled odour of smoke, cooking, dried meats and fish, and of human beings living in primitive and confined quarters. Cooking may well have been in progress, pots being among the embers and the refuse from the preparation of food lying about until it was dumped on the midden. In the right-hand corner, as today, there was a quern and there are also four watertight slab boxes set in the floor along the back of the room. One of these may have contained drinking water; salted meat or fish may have been soaking in a second; while one or both of the others may have been filled with shellfish which were either being softened for use as bait or de-gritted for human consumption. What would immediately attract the eye of the visitor would be the great stone dresser set in the rear wall. It is impressive enough today but would have been all the more so when its shelves were filled. In a painting of 1865 by John Cairns, RA, a large stone can be seen lying along the left edge of the hearth. This is no longer there but was probably a seat – which may have been rudely covered, even upholstered – and one can imagine some of the family being gathered around the hearth.

How many there were in this family is difficult to say. Anthropological parallels suggest that a structure with an area of 36 sq m might have housed anything from four people to four times that many. I think the best clue available, and that an indefinite one, is the answer given to a visitor to a small Orcadian house in 1847. He saw one box bed and wanted to know what the sleeping arrangements were for the parents and six children. They all slept in the same bed – and it measured 1.7 m by 1.2 m by 1.4 m! Some idea of the structure of the population of Orkney in neolithic times has been given and it is quite possible that the single house once accommodated not only parents and children but also unmarried siblings and such members of the older generation as had survived. The beds are there yet and are immediately recognisable for what they are to anyone familiar with the wooden box beds current for the last two centuries in Orkney and the stone ones which preceded them. There are possibly as many as five in all, each bounded by stone slabs on edge and occupying the sides of the room and the wall which contains the entrance. They are bare now but the defining stones would once have contained mattresses. It is usually held that these would have been of heather or straw but they may alternatively have been of the husks of grain – this being a traditional material – and it is not beyond the bounds of possibility that the down of eider ducks was employed, this being available from nests, as in Iceland. Skins must surely also have been used in bedding, covering the mattresses and serving in lieu of blankets. It can be seen that the occupants of house 1 at Skara Brae were comparatively well off; five beds for a family is a great deal more comfortable than one.

The description of the fixtures and fittings of the house has not quite been exhausted. Above some of the beds there were ambries or 'keeping places' and additionally there were originally four small cells leading off the main room, though only the two on the landward side now survive. That in the far right corner, now gone, is said to have had a drain in its floor which led seawards and Childe's suggestion that it was a family privy is a good one. There was another in the back wall which could be entered through the dresser while the third and fourth – still to be seen – are in the left-hand corner and between it and the entrance. It was from the last that the bolt was shot behind the door and it was the one in the left-hand corner which contained all the beads – this suggesting that such cells were used as places of safe-keeping. They may also have functioned as larders and as fuel stores, like the peat nooks of the recent past. In leaving the subject of Skara Brae two possibly linked phenomena might be mentioned – though there may be more. One is a series of three sockets ranged diagonally above the left principal bed of house 1 – they look rather as though they may have supported a staircase similar to those in the later brochs. The other is a doorway *over* the entrance of house 7. Is it conceivable that these houses had a complete or partial upper floor, even if only for a storage loft?

It is testimony to the richness of Orkney in neolithic remains that a whole settlement – Rinyo – can be passed over with little need for comment other than that it was very similar to Skara Brae – though much more ruinous. It is not visible now. The eight houses discovered may not all have been inhabited simultaneously and, in any case, must have only represented the end of a longer occupation since earlier midden was utilised to level terraces cut in the hillside to receive the known structures. Features of particular interest are that the slab drainage system – similar to that at Skara Brae – was lined with hazel bark and that one of the houses had next to its hearth the base of a clay oven which, doubtless, was domed when complete. Rinyo is another Grooved Ware settlement and a single date of 2385 (± 160) BC has now been obtained from bone surviving from the old excavations.

Skara Brae and Rinyo gave the impression that neolithic settlements in Orkney were very similar but it is now known that is not so. One of the most exciting discoveries of the past decade came with Anna Ritchie's recognition of Unstan Ware from the Knap of Howar. A series of radiocarbon determinations backed this up suggesting the site to have been occupied between 3602 and 2970 (± 200) BC, though there were traces of earlier activity. Again there is a long duration of settlement but the dates from the Knap of Howar are particularly exciting in that they provide the earliest indication of neolithic settlement in Orkney. Nothing is known of the original houses, samples having been taken from the midden below the later ones but even these later houses are remarkable in both date and preservation, being the best examples of domestic architecture that exist in Western Europe for such an early period (Pl. 23; Fig.

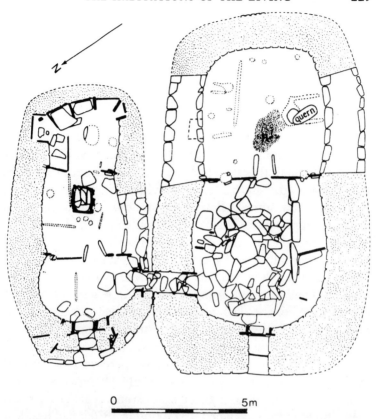

Fig. 45   The early neolithic houses at the Knap of Howar as excavated by Anna Ritchie

45). In contrast to Skara Brae and Rinyo the settlement seems never to have been a large one and though the two buildings which can be visited today are on the edge of the shore it is doubtful if there originally were any more. They are also of a distinctly different shape and Anna Ritchie has compared their hall-like proportions to those of the stalled tombs while considering the square rooms and side cells of Skara Brae and Rinyo to have more affinity with the Maes Howe variant. They do, however, have features in common, not the least of these being the recessing of the structures into earlier midden, the use of this material for packing in the walls, and the practice of heaping further refuse around the buildings after their erection.

The buildings at the Knap of Howar lie side by side, are joined by a connecting passage, each additionally having a separate entrance on their end nearest the shore. The largest and southernmost of the two is entered by a paved doorway, intentionally made long to baffle the wind, over which the lintels are still intact and where the inner door sill and jambs survive – though the latter have been damaged since they were first discovered. This building is divided into two rooms by a partition of four upright slabs of flagstone which runs across its transverse axis; posts between each outer pair of stones may have supported either the roof or the corbelling walls. The outer room was partially paved and still has against its right hand wall a low broad bench which may have served as a bed. The inner room, reached by a central gap in the partition, was unpaved, its floor having consisted of occupation material over the natural boulder clay. Grooves found in this subsoil suggest that there were benches or beds here, too, against both the right and left walls, these having been made of wood. There was also a central fireplace – this being just a circular ash-filled hollow – and, near it, a pot set in a hole and also a quernstone. The latter is still there and is enormous; when first found in 1930 it had beside it two rubbing stones and a quantity of broken razor shells. In this room, and indeed the building as a whole, there was only one aumbry, suggesting limited storage.

It is thought that the seaward entrance to the smaller of the two buildings was quickly blocked up and that it was thereafter entered through the passage from the larger, this, too, having had a door in it. This building is not only smaller but is divided into three rooms by transverse partitions. The first room, that nearest the sea, is featureless but the central one had a stone bench along its left-hand wall, which possibly replaced a wooden one, and has storage cupboards in its right-hand wall. In the centre of this room there was a fireplace, a simple, round, undefined hearth having succeeded a square stone one. In the case of the earlier fireplace a stone along its edge may have been a seat while four shallow hollows in the clay may have been to hold round-based pots. So far the two rooms are little different from those in the larger house and between them they indicate a formalised division of areas such as is only hinted at at Skara Brae and Rinyo. In this light the inner third room of the smallest building is of particular interest since it was intensively furnished with both flag-defined bays and wall cupboards and would appear to have functioned as a storage area. A central post hole here gives another clue to the manner in which the buildings were roofed.

In this survey of the known neolithic habitations of Orkney we come finally to the Links of Noltland. Both Skara Brae and the Knap of Howar have been rediscovered in an interpretive sense but the only knowledge that existed until recently of the Links of Noltland lay in the preserved manuscript notebooks of George Petrie. This antiquarian had found and investigated, to a slight extent, an exposed midden among the dunes at the north end of Westray on 20 September 1866. Though he likened it to Skara Brae at the time the potential of the site was appreciated only when his notebooks were being gone through with the republication of that site in mind. With the sudden awareness that a relatively untouched neolithic settlement existed somewhere on the Links of Noltland a small team was dispatched from the National Museum of Antiquities of Scotland in the summer of 1977. What they found was in some ways thrilling, and in other ways sad. Midden and some structures were discovered over an area of about 150 m by 50 m – four times that of Skara Brae – and test clearances proved the whole to relate to neolithic settlement of the Grooved Ware sub-culture. Unfortunately, however, the whole area was subject to erosion by the wind and sea, rabbit infestation, the trampling of cattle and the quarrying of sand; in places the neolithic midden simply lay bare and without protection.

Fencing was erected and government money made available

for four seasons of archaeological investigation under the direction of David Clarke. The problem – seemingly an insoluble one in the present financial climate – is that the funds are simply not available for the total excavation to present-day standards of a site of such importance and magnitude. Work had to be restricted to areas over two parts of the exposed midden and to a standing structure which has become known as Grobust. Some of the other important findings from the site as a whole have been mentioned elsewhere but it is Grobust which is of particular interest here. The building has features in common with others already known about – it is semi-subterranean and the cupboards and recesses built into its wall are familiar. It seems, however, to be quite unusual in both its shape and construction (Fig. 46). In the first place, it consists of two very irregular rooms joined by a covered passage some 3.5 m long. In the second, construction seems to have been on the basis of built pillars which were joined by masonry. Its exact nature – even whether it was a domestic structure – may lamentably never be known, as funding for the project was curtailed when the excavators had taken out only 1.5 m of the fill of the building, when the tops of the internal furnishings were just beginning to show. The reason for the slow progress made was in itself exciting, for the structure had not only been intentionally filled in but this had been done with selected materials in discrete deposits. There were dumps of varying types, some being rich in shell, others in bone, but they were unlike midden elsewhere, inclusions being fresh and unabraded. Moreover, artefacts were unusually common and were, again, in relatively good condition there being, among other things, hundreds of beads, a whalebone cup, a whole pot and a preponderance of pieces of decorated vessels. At the level at which excavation ceased part of one of the rooms could be seen to have been blocked off and seemingly associated with this was a whale rib, two cows' skulls and the carcass of an eagle.

What has been attempted in this and the preceding chapters has

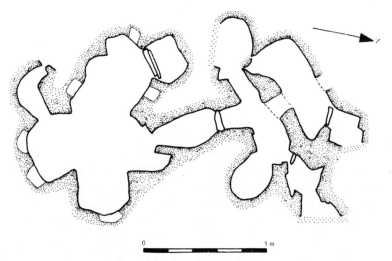

Fig. 46   The curious and complex structure at Grobust, Links of Noltland, as it has been so far revealed

been an overview of life in neolithic Orkney and it may seem strange to end it on such a note as Grobust – a partially excavated building, the structure, purpose and infilling of which are all enigmatic. It is, in fact, a very appropriate end. It is part of the excitement of the subject that prehistory – or, rather, our understanding of it – never stands still but is constantly open to reappraisal, both as a result of new discoveries and of fresh thinking. Isbister has certainly given us a clearer window on one part of tribal Britain in the New Stone Age than previously existed but there will be other sites – such as Grobust – that will extend our vision further still. It is a stimulating prospect made possible by an extraordinary richness of archaeological material and in this, as in other respects, Orkney is of intrinsic value to Europe's cultural heritage.

Epilogue · The Past in the Present

Many archaeological sites are excavated but few capture the popular imagination in the way that Isbister has. I have tried always to cater for the interest of the public in any work I have been connected with in the Northern Isles and such things as open-days, newspaper articles, local radio broadcasts and talks to local societies have brought a heartening response. With Isbister, however, matters have gone much, much further, and it has been difficult to keep pace with a growing interest which, so far, shows no signs of slackening. In the first few years following the excavations of 1976 I conducted a few organised visits for specially interested parties but even then the majority of those who came to the house of Ronnie and Morgan Simison had learnt of the discovery through the local media or by word of mouth. Some objects from the excavations had gone on display in Tankerness House Museum in Kirkwall in 1978, but in 1981 the curator, Bryce Wilson, devoted the whole of the Summer Exhibition to what was advertised as the 'Tomb of the Eagles'. This was a definite turning-point, for the display which he and his assistant, Anne Leith, put together was a great credit to themselves and could not fail to fire the interest of the public. Hundreds visited it and many subsequently found their way to the Simisons' door, having inquired en route for the 'Tomb of the Eagles'. It was a name that stuck and though Orkney Islands Council then erected signposts to 'Isbister Chambered Cairn' the Simisons have found it necessary to add other signs of their own making giving the site its popular title.

During this period I was working on various aspects of the more formal presentation of the excavations. Advance articles were subsequently printed in archaeological journals, lectures given at universities and, ultimately, in 1983 an academic monograph was published. The site featured in Anna and Graham Ritchie's *Scotland: Archaeology and Early History*; the Prehistoric Society's *Conference Guide to Orkney*; and will also appear in Audrey Henshall's chapter in *Prehistory of Orkney* edited by Colin Renfrew, and my own chapter in *The People of Orkney* edited by Sam Berry. It has become a key site in our understanding of prehistory – one that is likely to become as well known as Skara Brae, Brodgar and Maes Howe – and it must be said that there are things that can be learned from it yet.

The popular side of things has kept pace with all this. In 1982 Ronnie and Morgan Simison demurred at the suggestion that the site should be included in the brochure of the Orkney Tourist Organisation, though it was in that for South Ronaldsay and Burray; nevertheless, more than 500 people signed their visitors' book that year. The following year the ranks of sight-seers were swelled by popular bus tours from Kirkwall – there are over 1,000 entries in the book for 1983. Since then an excellent documentary by Howie Firth, Senior Producer of BBC Radio Orkney, has been networked, having been repeated twice, so far, on BBC Radio Scotland; a specially illustrated article by Roy Towers has appeared in the *Glasgow Herald*; the site has been photographed for the *National Geographic* magazine; and has been chosen by the BBC as a location for the televisation of one of George Mackay Brown's stories. The effect of this is that the number of visitors will increase yet further and one must spare a thought for Ronnie and Morgan Simison. They enjoy having visitors and have a passionate interest in the important and fascinating site which came to light as a result of their own initiative. The fact remains, nevertheless, that their livelihood depends on farming and the facilities they have are more geared to that than to the reception of hundreds, prospectively thousands, of callers.

One might ask why the site is not officially open to the public. In fact, the Simisons have very generously offered it to Orkney Islands Council if they will take it into guardianship. This is

now being considered and the tomb is of such importance
archaeologically and of such proven interest both to tourists and
to the populace of Orkney that the Council would do well to
take up the option. With the help of the Manpower Services
Commission and government youth schemes the tomb could be
restored to its former splendour, with the hornworks and cairn
being rebuilt under archaeological supervision. The information exists to permit this accurate reconstruction and the result
would be a monument of great scale and atmosphere; a fitting
tribute to those who colonised the islands so long ago. Nor must
the neighbouring burnt mound be forgotten for this is the only
house of its type and period – the Bronze Age – which is open to
the public, and its reconstruction would be a matter of comparative ease. The collection of objects from both sites should
be housed in a small, specially constructed museum at Liddle,
for preference a satellite of Tankerness House, and the exhibition there could be geared to the reception of large numbers of
visitors with information being displayed. All that would then
be required would be a tarmacadam road to the house, a carefully sited car park and a custodian – who, I hope, would be
either Ronnie or Morgan. The potential is there, it just needs to
be exploited, and at present moves are afoot to set up a Liddle &
Isbister Trust, the aim of which would be to promote the
reconstruction of the two sites and an increase in the facilities
available to visitors.

   That is, perhaps, for the future, but in the past, whether you
were the first visitor of the season or the last, there was a homely
welcome – as I'm sure there always will be. Some knock on the
door hesitantly but soon are within the house, as often as not
having a cup of tea or, if especially lucky, a taste of home-brew.
This is usually imbibed in a conservatory, built partly in order
to house a showcase donated by Tankerness House Museum,
and there is a distinct lack of formality, young children finding
plenty of toys with which to pass the time. Morgan shows the
visitors all the objects – which are housed at the farm – and tells
what she calls the 'story'. It is often very much a two-way

process, enthusiasm being infectious, and a visit to an ancient monument becomes an occasion of greater interest and duration than might ever have been imagined. Archaeological matters are discussed and opinions exchanged, the conversation centring on what the visitors want to know as much as anything else; the privileged are even allowed to handle objects of particular interest to them. The information the Simisons derive from their visitors is as wide-ranging as the places they come from – in the visitors' book there are addresses in the United States, Canada, Fiji, Japan, Korea, Italy, France, West Germany, Scandinavia, Zimbabwe, The Netherlands, Belgium, Iran, Lebanon and, of course, from different parts of Britain. One person was even told of the site in Australia! It was perhaps this visitor who told Morgan that Aborigines there still lay their dead out on bushes until the bones are clean and dry; and an American woman related that the North American Indians give pots a new lease of life by drilling and binding them – comparable holes in the Isbister pottery are there to be seen. Such involvement is surely what – in an ideal world – all museums should aim for; the number of letters and presents the Simisons receive from past visitors is testimony to its effectiveness – though it has to be admitted that the charm of the Simisons is a major ingredient in the success of the enterprise. Certainly, visits are enjoyed by groups of pupils from various schools in Orkney – there was also a party from a school in Aberdeenshire for the mentally handicapped; as Morgan has said, 'I wish history lessons had been like that when I was a bairn.'

But the visit is not yet over. Ronnie has appeared, there being an interval in the farm work, and the visitors walk off with him – sometimes in borrowed boots and waterproofs – and usually in the company of the farm dog. On occasion, when Ronnie is busy, the dog alone goes – for he knows the way. It has happened that he has led visitors in the wrong direction, though; Ronnie puts it down to the dog's sense of humour. Anyway, the walk to the cliffs is broken half-way by a visit to the burnt mound. From there the tomb is visible as only a slight rise silhouetted against the sky on the coastline and it must be said that it is not until one walks over the top of it that it becomes truly impressive. There is the chamber, to be crawled about at will and, on either side, the rise of the land curves round a bowl of flagstones whose eastward side drops sheer into the crashing sea. I have been told by members of the public – and I believe it – that there is nothing quite like being taken around an archaeological monument by its excavator. Everything is so fresh and immediate and I am sure that the privileged visitor to Isbister must almost relive the investigation with Ronnie as a guide.

When in Orkney I sometimes walk down to the tomb of Isbister to spend time on my own. It is a place of great atmosphere where, cut off from the outside world, one is inescapably made aware of the past. I am not talking of psychic phenomena here but, more mundanely, of the sheer impressiveness of a prehistoric monument and the insight which modern archaeology can give us into the period in which it was built. One can almost bring it to life in the imagination and even in its present state of decay it provokes considerable reflection. Perhaps one day it will be the source of inspiration for a piece of music – the thought itself is an indication of my feelings. But what of the sea eagles? Those majestic birds which have captured the popular imagination. They have been successfully reintroduced to Britain – on Rhum by John Love of the Nature Conservancy Council – and it is hoped that eggs will hatch for the first time in 1984. Perhaps as exciting, a white-tailed sea eagle was recorded in 1983 by Kevin Woodbridge in North Ronaldsay and in the spring of 1984 two other local ornithologists, John and Bobby McCutcheon, sighted one in South Ronaldsay. It is not an impossibility that the white-tailed sea eagle will nest once more on the cliffs below the tomb of Isbister.

Bibliography

This is intended as a brief list of recommended reading and not as an exhaustive compilation of references used. The books listed, and particularly *Isbister*, give access to most source information.

Berry, R.J. (ed.), *The People of Orkney*, Stromness. From prehistory to the present day. To be published 1984.

Fenton, A., *The Northern Isles*, Edinburgh, 1978. A sourcebook of information on traditional life in Orkney and Shetland.

Fraser, D., *Land and Society in Neolithic Orkney*, Oxford, 1983. A view from a geographical perspective.

Hedges, J.W., *Isbister: A Chambered Tomb in Orkney*. Oxford, 1983. The academic publication.

Henshall, A.S., *The Chambered Tombs of Scotland*, Vol 1, Edinburgh, 1963. Encyclopaedic.

Love, J.A., *The Return of the Sea Eagle*, Cambridge, 1983. The reintroduction of sea eagles to Rhum by the Nature Conservancy Council.

Marwick, E.W., *The Folklore of Orkney and Shetland*, London, 1975. The best book on a fascinating subject.

Renfrew, C., *Before Civilization*, London, 1973. The New Archaeology.

Renfrew, C., *Investigations in Orkney*, London, 1979. Quanterness, Maes Howe, Brodgar – and theory.

Renfrew, C. (ed.), *The Prehistory of Orkney*, Edinburgh. A complete and up-to-date review. To be published 1984.

Ritchie, A. & Ritchie, J.N.G., *The Ancient Monuments of Orkney*, Edinburgh, 1978. An invaluable booklet to have by one in Orkney.

Sahlins, M.D., *Tribesmen*, New Jersey, 1968. A compact and clear grounding.

Shearer, J. et al., *The New Orkney Book*, London, 1966. Published for Orkney schools and gives a comprehensive view.

Astro-archaeology: Thom, A., *Megalithic Sites in Britain*, Oxford, 1967; *Megalithic Lunar Observatories*, Oxford, 1971; Thom, A. & Thom, A.S., *Megalithic Remains in Britain and Brittany*, Oxford, 1978.

Palaeodemography: Acsádi, G.Y. & Nemeskeri, J., *History of Human Lifespan and Mortality*, Budapest, 1970; Hassan, F.A., On mechanisms of population growth during the neolithic, *Current Anthropology*, Vol 14, 1973, 535–42; Weiss, K.M. *Demographic Models for Anthropology* (=*American Antiquity*, Vol 38, 1973, no.2, pt.2).

Index